# INSPIRING TRUE STORIES FOR GIRLS—SPORTS EDITION

EXPLORE THE AMAZING JOURNEYS OF 15 INCREDIBLE FEMALE ATHLETES - WITH VALUABLE LIFE LESSONS TO INSPIRE, EMPOWER, AND BUILD CONFIDENCE IN GIRLS

STELLA BRIGHT

© **Copyright 2024 - All rights reserved.**

The content contained within this book may not be reproduced, duplicated or transmitted without direct written permission from the author or the publisher.

Under no circumstances will any blame or legal responsibility be held against the publisher, or author, for any damages, reparation, or monetary loss due to the information contained within this book, either directly or indirectly.

Legal Notice:

This book is copyright protected. It is only for personal use. You cannot amend, distribute, sell, use, quote or paraphrase any part, or the content within this book, without the consent of the author or publisher.

Disclaimer Notice:

Please note the information contained within this document is for educational and entertainment purposes only. All effort has been executed to present accurate, up to date, reliable, complete information. No warranties of any kind are declared or implied. Readers acknowledge that the author is not engaged in the rendering of legal, financial, medical or professional advice. The content within this book has been derived from various sources. Please consult a licensed professional before attempting any techniques outlined in this book.

By reading this document, the reader agrees that under no circumstances is the author responsible for any losses, direct or indirect, that are incurred as a result of the use of the information contained within this document, including, but not limited to, errors, omissions, or inaccuracies.

✨ *Girls with Grit & Grace* ✨

## *Grit*

Have the determination and courage to continue doing something even though it is very difficult

## *Grace*

Behave in a pleasant, polite, and dignified way, even when upset or being treated unfairly

Collins Dictionary definitions 2024

# CONTENTS

*Introduction*   vii

1. Venus and Serena Williams   1
2. Marta Vieira da Silva   11
3. Lindsey Vonn   19
4. Hayley Wickenheiser   27
5. Tamika Catchings   37
6. Annika Sörenstam   47
7. Simone Biles   57
8. DeeDee Trotter   69
9. Katie Ledecky   79
10. Mia Hamm   87
11. Danica Patrick   97
12. Dame Sarah Storey   105
13. Leticia Bufoni   117
14. Bethany Hamilton   127

*Conclusion*   135
*Glossary*   140
*About the Author*   141
*References / Further Reading / Listening*   142

# INTRODUCTION

Hey there! Welcome to a world where girls take on challenges, face their fears, and achieve incredible things. Are you ready to follow in the footsteps of 15 girls with incredible grit and grace: ordinary girls who, through hard work, determination, and courage, became extraordinary?

For far too long, we've heard countless stories about male sports stars – how they scored the winning shot, swam faster than anyone else, or ran so quickly they left everyone else behind. But what about the incredible girls who have rocked the sports world? This book is all about them. It's high time we celebrated their journeys, triumphs, and remarkable stories. And here's the best part: they started just like you, with huge dreams. With courage, fierce determination, and hard work, they turned those dreams into spectacular successes.

The world of women's sports has changed so much over the last 20 years. Can you believe there was a time, not so long ago, when girls were often discouraged or even banned from playing many sports because they were seen as "just for boys?" Thankfully, some incredible female athletes have shown the world what girls are made of! They have broken down barriers and crushed old stereotypes, helping ensure every girl who dreams of excelling in any sport, even those once reserved for boys, has the chance to shine.

In this book, you'll find stories of women who are global celebrities, as well as those who might not be as famous but whose stories are equally inspiring. You'll learn about their beginnings, the hurdles they faced, and how they came out stronger on the other side. As you turn these pages, remember that these stories are about real people who started off just like you. They had dreams, doubts, successes, and failures. You'll discover that the road to success wasn't always smooth for them. Each faced her own set of challenges, setbacks, and moments of unhappiness. What sets them apart is their unwavering determination to keep going, push beyond their limits, and never give up, no matter how hard things get.

Their stories are about much more than winning gold medals, lifting trophies, or crossing the finish line first; they are filled with valuable life lessons and secrets to success that extend far beyond sports – from working hard and never giving up to facing your fears and learning from mistakes. Whether your dream is to be a sports superstar, a heart-stirring musician, a master chef, or a groundbreaking scientist, this book will show you that no dream is too big and that anything is possible if you put your mind to it.

I was inspired to write *Inspiring True Stories for Girls—Sports Edition* because I believe every girl has what it takes to do amazing things. Sometimes, we just need a sprinkle of encouragement and inspiration to help us on our way! From tennis courts to skate parks and soccer fields to the vast ocean, the following pages are filled with tales of girls who kicked, paddled, and raced their way to make their dreams a reality. So, buckle up and get ready to be inspired.

Happy reading, and remember, you can achieve incredible things!

# 1

# VENUS AND SERENA WILLIAMS

"It doesn't matter what your background is or where you come from, if you have dreams and goals, that's all that matters."

Serena Williams

"You have to believe in yourself when no-one else does - that makes you a winner right there."

Venus Williams

I magine a world where you're judged simply by how you look, your skin color, and where you grew up. Now, meet two sisters who lived in that world but rose above it to become icons and legends. This is the story of the Williams sisters – Venus and Serena, and their journey from the rough streets of Compton, California, to the beautiful tennis courts of Wimbledon and Flushing Meadows. They defied all the odds, overcoming adversity, breaking barriers, and showing that talent combined with hard work can lead to extraordinary success. Their story is one of grit, determination, and unwavering support from their family.

Venus Ebony Starr Williams was born on June 17, 1980, in Lynwood, California, and her sister Serena Jameka Williams followed a little over a year later, on September 26, 1981. They were the youngest of five sisters. Their mother, Oracene, was a nurse, and their father, Richard, owned a security service company. In 1983, the family moved to Compton, California, a tough neighborhood with a high crime rate.

One day, Richard was watching a tennis tournament on television and realized that top female tennis players could earn thousands of dollars by playing in tournaments. This sparked an idea: what if he coached his daughters to become tennis superstars? And so, it all started. Serena began playing tennis with her big sister, Venus, when she was only three years old.

Richard Williams had no formal training as a tennis coach, but that didn't stop him: he read every book he could find, watched videos to learn new techniques, talked to experts, and did everything he could to be the best coach for his daughters. He was a loving parent but also a strict coach when it came to playing tennis. For hours every day, Venus and Serena trained relentlessly under his guidance. They weren't just learning tennis skills; they were also building mental toughness and the belief that they could achieve anything they set their minds to.

Richard took Venus and Serena to train at the local tennis courts in a run-down park. There was often broken glass on the courts, people drinking and taking drugs nearby, and sometimes, they could hear gunshots in the distance as they practiced. He wanted them to see how tough life could be and understand that they could rise above their circumstances with hard work, determination, and resilience.

A few years later, the Williams family moved to Florida so Venus and Serena could train at the prestigious Rick Macci Tennis Academy, which has shaped many successful tennis players. The Academy offered better training facilities and more opportunities to compete against other talented young players. Rick Macci recognized both girls' raw talent and potential, pushing them to reach new heights. It was both an exciting and challenging time for Venus and Serena.

At this time, tennis was a predominantly White and affluent sport; Serena and Venus were frequently viewed as outsiders. They often endured prejudice and negativity from the media, coaches, other players, and their families. Hurtful comments about their appearance, race, and even their unique playing style became a part of their everyday life on and off the court. However, rather than letting the comments discourage them, they used the criticism to fuel their determination. The negativity motivated them both to work even harder to prove others wrong and show that anyone can break barriers with passion and dedication. For Venus and Serena, the criticism didn't just help them develop thicker skin; it also strengthened their bond as sisters. Facing challenges together brought them closer. They became each other's biggest cheerleaders, sharing not only their triumphs but also their struggles and setbacks.

As the girls continued to improve and win more matches, Richard made the controversial decision to withdraw his daughters from the junior tennis circuit for a while. Venus and Serena were facing significant criticism, prejudice, and negativity, and he worried about their mental health. He decided they needed a break from competitive tennis to focus on their schoolwork and enjoy their childhood. They continued to train for long hours but away from the media spotlight.

Venus turned professional in 1994, and Serena followed a year later, embarking on journeys that would see them shatter expectations and change tennis forever. They quickly became known for their incredible skills; they played the game like no one else on the tour—powerful, strong, and fearless. This was something new in women's tennis, especially coming from such young competitors, and it inspired awe and admiration all around.

The early years of their careers were marked by numerous defeats. In her first tournament as a professional, Venus won her first match but was defeated in the second round. Serena lost her first professional match in straight sets. Instead of being discouraged, Venus and Serena treated each loss as a valuable learning experience. They learned that every setback carried a lesson, and every lesson was a step toward improvement. Serena has said, *"I've grown most not from victories but setbacks."*

A match that taught Venus a life-changing lesson was the semi-final of the US Open, a Grand Slam event, in 1999 when she was just 19. Grand Slams or Majors are the four big, most prestigious tennis tournaments (the Australian Open, the French Open, Wimbledon, and the US Open), and winning one is a significant achievement. Venus was desperate to win her first Grand Slam title and faced Martina Hingis, a formidable opponent. Venus remembers wanting to win badly but hoping to do so through Hingis making mistakes rather than pushing herself to play better. Hingis didn't make enough mistakes and won the match. This defeat was incredibly tough for Venus, but it turned out to be a pivotal moment in her journey. Venus realized that if she wanted to achieve greatness, she couldn't rely on others making errors; she had to take full responsibility for her performance and put in the extra effort to become the best.

In the same tournament, Martina Hingis went on to play Serena in the final. Serena won the match, becoming US Open champion and securing her first Grand Slam title aged 17 and 350 days.

Venus was determined not to let another opportunity slip away and trained harder than ever. The following year, her efforts paid off spectacularly when she won not one but two Grand Slam titles, claiming victory at both Wimbledon and the US Open.

Time and again, Venus and Serena wowed the tennis world with their incredible skills, power, and mental toughness, often sweeping through tournaments to play against each other in major finals. The professional rivalry between Venus and Serena Williams is legendary, marked by intense matches that pushed each sister to her limits. Whether practicing or playing in big matches, they pushed each other to run faster, hit harder, and think smarter. Being such fierce opponents on the court could easily have led to feelings of jealousy and resentment. Yet, Venus and Serena always supported each other unconditionally, acknowledging that their success would not have been possible without the other.

Over the course of her career, Venus won seven Grand Slam singles titles, including five Wimbledon championships. She also boasts fourteen major doubles titles, often partnering with Serena, and four Olympic gold medals.

Serena's trophy shelf is bursting with Grand Slam titles—23 in singles, the most by any player in the Open Era. She has an achievement named after her—the Serena Slam—which involves winning four Grand Slams in a row. Additionally, Serena has won 14 Grand Slam women's doubles titles, 2 mixed doubles Grand Slams, and four Olympic gold medals.

Their achievements are truly extraordinary, but they have both faced their share of challenges over the years. In the early stages of their careers, Venus and Serena struggled to escape negative comments about their race, physique, and background. Radio personalities, TV broadcasters, and newspaper journalists made hurtful comments about their appearance. Fellow competitors often mocked them in front of thousands of people at tournaments.

Serena is quoted as saying, *"It was hard for me; people would say I was born a guy, all because of my arms, or because I'm strong"*.

However, Venus and Serena refused to let the hate and negativity define them. They understood that these comments didn't reflect their true selves and channeled the criticism into a powerful drive to succeed, all while maintaining grace and sportsmanship. By choosing to turn the negativity into a positive force, the sisters not only proved their critics wrong but also inspired girls and women worldwide to do the same.

Venus and Serena have suffered serious health issues and injuries, forcing them to take breaks from tennis to rest and recover. Injuries might seem like huge obstacles, but for Venus and Serena Williams, they were opportunities to come back even stronger. Each time they got hurt, the sisters didn't just rest; they followed tough rehab programs, tried out new fitness routines, and worked on building their strength and stamina. This hard work meant that when Venus and Serena returned to the tennis court, they were not just ready to play— they were better than ever. In an interview after the 2013 French Open, Serena explained, *"I think I've always said a champion isn't about how much they win, but it's about how they recover from their downs, whether it's an injury or whether it's a loss."*

In addition to on-court injuries, Venus struggled with health issues that threatened to derail her career completely. She suffered from severe joint pain and fatigue, which were later diagnosed as symptoms of Sjögren's Syndrome. On days when she could only train for a few minutes, Venus focused on what she could do rather than her limitations. Her determination led to a revamped diet and training regimen that allowed her to manage her symptoms and continue competing.

Venus and Serena's resilience teaches us an invaluable lesson about perseverance. Facing setbacks, whether in tennis, school, or life, can be tough, but overcoming them is what truly defines us. Their journeys show that with determination and hard work, obstacles can be transformed into stepping stones for success.

The Williams sisters' impact now stretches well beyond the tennis courts. Venus combines her love for fashion and design through her clothing line, EleVen, and her interior design company, V Starr Interiors. Serena has founded a fashion label, a skincare brand, and Serena Ventures, which invests in companies led by women and minorities, promoting greater diversity in the business sector. Together, they engage in extensive charity work, supporting educational initiatives, youth programs, and community development projects. Their involvement in these efforts sends a clear message to the world: everyone deserves a shot at success, no matter what their starting point. Both women actively support and fight for gender equality in sport. Venus played a pivotal role in the campaign for equal prize money for female athletes, leading to significant changes in tennis tournaments worldwide.

Despite their fame and incredible success, Venus and Serena have never forgotten their roots. In their hometown of Compton, California, they founded a charity to support families affected by violence, offering them hope and practical help. This project was sparked by personal tragedy following the devastating loss of their half-sister, Yetunde, to gun violence.

Let's take a moment to appreciate Venus and Serena not just as legendary athletes but as trailblazers who redefined what's possible. Together, they changed the face of women's tennis, making it more popular and respected than ever before. They opened up the sport to girls everywhere, showing them that they, too, can achieve greatness, no matter what their background.

### *Instances of Grit & Grace:*

### *Grit:*

- The endless hours they spent on court, honing their skills and building their strength.
- The countless sessions spent in rehab to overcome injuries and comeback stronger than ever.
- Their unwavering determination to keep going, refusing to give up despite the negativity and prejudice they faced.

### *Grace:*

- Despite their fierce rivalry on the court, Serena and Venus have always supported each other. Their ability to put family

first and share joy in each other's achievements shows true sisterly love and grace.
- The way they dealt with all the unfair criticism and bias they faced throughout their career – responding calmly and staying composed even when times were tough.
- Never forgetting their roots and using their fame and success to help others, showing true champions use their celebrity to make the world a better place. In Serena's words: *"Make sure you're very courageous: be strong, be extremely kind, and above all, be humble."*

*Key Life Lessons:*

- **Believe in Your Own Beauty:** Venus and Serena taught us that diversity is beautiful. You are unique and wonderful regardless of your skin color, body shape, or where you come from. Always be proud of who you are and celebrate your differences.
- **Turn Negativity into Strength:** The Williams sisters showed us that negative comments from others can be transformed into motivation. Don't let others define you. Instead, use their doubts as fuel to prove them wrong and shine in your own way.
- **Work Hard and Believe in Yourself:** Venus and Serena's story shows us that any goal is achievable with hard work and belief. Even when others doubted them, their self-belief was unshakeable. As Venus has said: *"Just believe in yourself. Even if you don't, pretend that you do and, at some point, you will."*
- **Don't Fear Failure:** Venus and Serena learned from their defeats and failures, seeing them as opportunities to grow stronger and smarter.

The stories of Venus and Serena Williams are not just about tennis; they're about the relentless pursuit of excellence, the courage to fight for equality, and the determination to turn dreams into reality. Their journeys teach us that no matter where we start, with resilience, hard work, and a commitment to taking responsibility for our successes and failures, we can achieve extraordinary things. Their story is a powerful reminder that even in a world full of hurdles, with the right mindset and support, anyone can achieve their dreams. Let's take inspiration from Venus's words:

*"I've learned that you can always achieve more than you thought you could. There are moments when I've walked off the court, and I'm like, I don't know how I won that match.' It was actually impossible, but it happened, and then you realize that you can push yourself much further than you ever thought, and you can make the impossible happen."*

Now get ready to journey to Brazil to meet our next sporting superstar...

# 2

## MARTA VIEIRA DA SILVA

"We all have obstacles. The feeling of satisfaction comes from overcoming something"

Marta Vieira da Silva

Join us on an incredible journey with Marta Vieira da Silva, a tale of growth and triumph that begins in the lively streets of Brazil and spans the world's soccer fields. This is a story of how a young girl from a modest background became an international icon and global soccer sensation against all odds. As we explore Marta's path, you'll discover how creativity, perseverance, and resilience can turn dreams into reality. Whether you're a soccer fan or not, Marta's story will empower and inspire you.

Marta was born on February 19, 1986, in a small rural town in Brazil, a country renowned for its breathtaking beaches, dense forests, and colorful festivals—a country with a deep love for soccer. In Marta's town, people often lacked access to food and money to support their families. Many children, especially girls, were not fortunate enough to attend school.

Marta's father left when she was a baby, leaving her mom, Tereza, to raise Marta and her three siblings alone. Tereza worked long hours—juggling jobs on a plantation and cleaning at city hall to support her family. Marta was deeply inspired by her mother's strength and determination, and to this day, she credits Tereza for teaching her resilience and instilling a strong work ethic.

Marta loved soccer from an early age. Watching her two brothers play, she longed to join them. To Marta, soccer was more than a game; it was a passion that filled her soul with joy and offered an escape from the realities of everyday life.

However, pursuing her passion was not easy. Most people in her town thought only boys should play soccer. Girls were expected to play with dolls and stay away from the rough and tumble of sports. Even her brothers didn't think she should play football. This left Marta feeling confused and frustrated. After all, why did being a girl have to stop her from playing the game she loved? In a letter to her younger self, she writes: *'Growing up in a small town like Dois Riachos, you stood out. But not for your talent. No, you got weird looks and mean comments every day just because you were a girl. A girl who loved football.'*

Marta refused to give up. She watched Brazilian legends like Ronaldo and Rivaldo, eagerly learning and incorporating their skills into her gameplay. Often playing without shoes, she molded grocery bags into soccer balls and used abandoned, deflated balls she found lying around. No other girls in her town wanted to play soccer, so she often spent hours practicing on her own. Sometimes, the boys let her play with them but always put her on the team with less skilled players.

Eventually, she was allowed to join the local boys' football team. It was a lonely time for her, being the only girl on the team. She had to change alone in a small bathroom while the boys chatted and had fun in the next-door locker room. On one occasion, she was pulled from the lineup because the opposing coach refused to play against a girl. She recalls the tears welling up in her eyes.

Still, she refused to give up on her dreams, using the injustice to strengthen her resolve and prove all the doubters wrong.

Speaking about her childhood, Marta has said, *"There were many obstacles; my mother raised all her children by herself and couldn't afford football boots for me. But I've never lost the drive to win, to pursue my dreams."*

Her mom and grandmother refused to listen to those criticizing Marta and encouraged her not to give up on her dreams. With their support, her love for football grew even stronger.

The turning point in Marta's life came when she was 14 years old. While playing with the local boys' team, a coach from Rio de Janeiro, Brazil's former capital city, noticed her incredible talent. He asked if she would consider moving to Rio to join a newly formed women's team. At age 14, Marta had to make a huge decision: should she leave her family and move to a city she had never visited?

With her heart full of dreams, she packed a bag and boarded a bus to Rio. She later wrote about this in her letter to her younger self:

*"Don't think about it...How scared you are...How nervous you are... How everyone has said you can't do it... That you shouldn't do it...*

*Don't think about any of that.*

*Just get on the bus."*

Getting on the bus and facing her fears was a huge step for Marta, setting her on the path to fulfilling her dreams.

In Rio, Marta's soccer career would truly begin. The challenges were immense—adapting to city life, handling homesickness, struggling with shyness and more hurtful comments – now from older city girls —but Marta's resilience shone through.

At her trial for the Vasco da Gama women's team, Marta focused on her soccer skills, determined to impress the coaches and fellow players. Her talent amazed everyone watching, and they quickly recognized her incredible potential. Marta was signed to the team, and her reputation as a formidable player rapidly grew.

Marta stayed with Vasco for two seasons before transferring to Santa Cruz. In 2004, she moved to Europe, joining the Swedish club Umeå. In her first season, she helped the team win the UEFA Women's Cup title (now the UEFA Women's Champions League) and reach the finals in 2007 and 2008. In her second season, she scored 21 goals, Umeå was undefeated and claimed the league title. Her team went on to win the league title for four consecutive years, from 2005 to 2008. Over her five seasons with Umeå, Marta scored 111 goals in 103 league matches and was the leading goal scorer three times in 2004, 2005, and 2008. Her playing style—characterized by exceptional agility, sharp intelligence, and a unique ability to read the game—made her a standout player.

In 2009, Marta left Europe to play with the Los Angeles Sol in the Women's Professional Soccer (WPS) league, where she earned the Most Valuable Player (MVP) title. After the Sol folded, she joined FC Gold Pride, leading them to a WPS championship and winning her second MVP award in 2010. Marta returned to Brazil to play for Santos FC in Brazil during WPS off-seasons in 2009 and 2010. In 2011, she won another WPS title with the Western New York Flash. Marta then returned to Sweden, playing for Tyresö FF in 2012, and later moved to FC Rosengård in 2014. In 2017, she moved back to the US, signing for the Orlando Pride.

Marta had a golden international career with Brazil. In 2002, she joined the Brazilian women's national team. At 17, she played in her first FIFA World Cup for Brazil, scoring a penalty in their opening match against the Republic of Korea. At the 2007 Women's World Cup, she won the Golden Boot by scoring seven goals during the tournament and led Brazil to a second-place finish.

During her career, she shattered expectations and set new records, including becoming the top scorer in FIFA World Cup tournaments for both women and men. Marta scored 17 goals in World Cup tournaments, just ahead of the top male scorer, Miroslav Klose, who scored 16. Marta was named FIFA World Player of the Year five consecutive times from 2006 to 2010 and again in 2018.

Additionally, Marta helped Brazil secure Olympic silver medals in 2004 and 2008. At the Tokyo Games, Marta became the first footballer to score in five consecutive Olympic tournaments, although Brazil lost in the quarterfinals. In April 2024, Marta announced that she would retire from international competition after the Olympic Games in Paris. Brazil lost to the US in the final, earning Marta her third Olympic silver medal.

At the Maracanã Stadium in Rio de Janeiro, there is a sidewalk of fame featuring footprints of Brazilian footballing legends. In 2018, Marta became the first (and to date, only) woman to add her footprints. Her inclusion is a huge step toward raising the profile of women's football in Brazil and around the world.

Marta's influence extends beyond the soccer field. From a very young age, Marta dreamed of becoming a role model for girls around the globe, the role model she wished for as a child. In 2018, Marta was appointed as a UN Women Goodwill Ambassador, a role through which she champions equal opportunities for girls in sports worldwide. Her message is clear: no matter the obstacles, with determination and support, girls can achieve greatness. Whatever your dream, Marta teaches us that with creativity—like turning grocery bags into soccer balls—and the courage to believe in yourself, any barrier can be overcome.

***Instances of Grit & Grace:***

***Grit:***

- Refusing to give up on her dream of playing soccer despite no other girls playing when she was growing up. In Marta's words: *"Never give up on your dreams. The road may be a little difficult, but never give up."*
- Leaving her hometown and moving to Rio de Janeiro when she was fourteen.

***Grace:***

- The way she dealt with the gender bias and hurtful comments she faced growing up – choosing to let her soccer skills do the talking.
- Showing remarkable sportsmanship, even in defeat. She's known for consoling her teammates after disappointing losses and gracefully congratulating the victors, putting her own feelings to one side.
- Using her voice passionately and positively to champion equal opportunities for girls in sports worldwide

***Key Life Lessons:***

- **Push through your Fears**: Marta left her small town to pursue her dreams in a city despite feeling nervous and scared. Real growth often happens when you step outside your comfort zone and do things that feel scary.
- **Follow Your Heart:** Marta's love for soccer shone brightly, even when she had little support. Do things that make you happy, and don't let anyone discourage you from doing what you love.

- **Find Creative Ways to Overcome Obstacles**: Faced with no proper equipment, Marta made soccer balls from grocery bags. When you encounter barriers, think outside the box and use your creativity to find solutions.
- **Stand Up for Your Rights:** Despite facing gender bias, Marta never gave up on her dreams. Always stand up for your right to participate and excel in any field, regardless of what people say.

Marta's story is more than just a tale of soccer; it's a narrative of incredible resilience, the power of dreams, and the bravery to overcome barriers. Her journey teaches us that no matter what your background, you can reach spectacular heights with determination, creativity, and the strength to push through challenges. So, take a leaf out of Marta's book—embrace every challenge, harness every setback as a stepping stone, and never doubt your ability to make your dreams come true.

We're now travelling to the snowy mountains of the United States to meet a skiing legend. Her story is a true example of resilience and determination.

# 3

## LINDSEY VONN

"If you go around being afraid, you're never going to enjoy life. You have only one chance, so you've got to have fun"

Lindsey Vonn

In this story, we'll race down mountains and tackle icy challenges, falling and getting up again. Lindsey Vonn's life is a thrilling tale of speed, strength, and spirit that extends far beyond the snowy slopes she loved. Her life isn't just about flying down hills on skis at crazy speeds or collecting gold medals. Sure, those moments are super cool, but there's much more to her story. It delves into the tough and not-so-glamorous side of following your dreams. We'll learn about the power of perseverance, the importance of mental health, and the courage it takes to bounce back from injuries and setbacks and push even harder.

Born on October 18, 1984, in Minnesota, Lindsey grew up in a close-knit family of six. Though Minnesota is not known for towering peaks, its snowy winters provided the perfect backdrop for Lindsey's future in skiing. Unfortunately, her mom suffered a stroke during Lindsey's birth and never fully recovered. Despite being unable to join the family in activities like biking or skiing, she remained incredibly positive. This enduring optimism deeply inspired Lindsey, particularly during her battles with injuries and sadness.

From her earliest years, Lindsey was drawn to the thrill of skiing and the beauty of the mountains, a passion passed down from her father and grandfather, both keen, competitive skiers. At just three years old, Lindsey took to the slopes, tumbling and getting back up, learning the importance of resilience. Initially, Lindsey wasn't the fastest on her skis; her first coach even nicknamed her the 'turtle' during her debut race! However, with his coaching and her family's unwavering support, she worked tirelessly to improve. This dedication transformed her from a cautious beginner to a legendary icon in downhill skiing.

Aged seven, Lindsey competed in her first skiing tournament. By the age of nine, she was competing internationally. That same year, she met her skiing idol, Picabo Street, an Olympic gold medalist and World Cup champion, at a book signing event. Lindsey recalls the life-changing meeting in her autobiography *Rise*: *"I met her at an auto-graph signing ... and she changed my life. I went home that night and told my dad I wanted to be in the Olympics."*

Once Lindsey's dad made sure she understood the hard work and sacrifices required, they worked together to create a ten-year plan that would take Lindsey to the Olympics.

As Lindsey grew up, her rigorous training became more serious. She and her mother traveled across states so she could train at the prestigious Ski Club Vail. It was a sixteen-hour journey from Minnesota, with Lindsey often asleep in the back while her mother drove through the night, singing.

In the late '90s, the family moved to Vail, Colorado, to avoid the long journeys and ensure Lindsey could train more intensively. While Lindsey loved the intense training and spending so much time on the slopes, she missed out on some traditional childhood activities. Whether it was sleepovers, school dances, or making new friends, her strict schedule and tiring sports routine didn't leave much room for a typical youth.

In 1999, aged 14, Lindsey made history at the Trofeo Topolino in Italy, becoming the first American girl to win the prestigious slalom race for skiers aged 11–14. This victory was just the beginning; her impressive performances in numerous international races secured her a place at the 2002 Olympic Winter Games when she was only 17. She raced in the slalom and combined events in Salt Lake City, coming sixth in the combined. A year later, she won silver in downhill at the Junior World Championships in France.

As Lindsey's career was starting to take off, she faced a major setback. During a practice session for the 2006 Olympics, she had a serious crash and had to be taken to hospital. Despite the bruises and pain, she was determined to compete. After spending just two days recovering, she was back on the slopes. Although Lindsey didn't win any Olympic medals that year, her courage and resilience didn't go unnoticed. She received the US Olympic Spirit Award, becoming the first woman to receive this honor without a medal win.

Lindsey's career is a montage of breathtaking highs and painful lows. She is one of the most decorated alpine skiers in history: her wins include four World Cup overall titles (2008, 2009, 2010, and 2012), securing her place as one of the sport's legends. Lindsey claimed 82 World Cup victories, the most by any female skier, and won Olympic gold in the downhill at the 2010 Vancouver Games, as well as two Olympic bronze medals (2010, 2018). In addition, she has eight World Championship medals, two of which are gold.

However, her career was marked by numerous painful injuries that would make most people want to quit - serious knee problems, broken bones, and countless hours in rehab. Lindsey chose to see these setbacks as opportunities to get back up and push even harder. Her determination to keep going isn't just about skiing: it teaches us all a valuable lesson about persevering through tough times.

When asked in an interview about her various injuries, Lindsey smiled brightly and shared how thankful she was to have had the chance to pursue her passion for skiing and the joy it had brought her for so many years. She used her mother's story as inspiration to help her come back from her injuries – feeling grateful that her body would allow her to heal and recover. Lindsey's story is a perfect example of how staying positive can transform how we see our challenges.

The challenges Lindsey faced weren't only physical. Apart from the bruises and broken bones, she also had to deal with depression triggered by her injuries, the intensive rehabilitation sessions, and the frustration of not being able to compete in some major competitions. There were days when her coaches would have to drag her out of bed to train.

Lindsey also faced pressure from the media. Some critics suggested her success was more about her looks than her abilities on the slopes. Others claimed she exaggerated or even fabricated her injuries to gain media attention.

It's super important to remember how big a deal mental health is and how it can affect everything you do. Lindsey didn't tell her family about her depression for about ten years and admits it felt like a huge weight had been lifted from her shoulders when she finally told people how she was feeling. She is now very open about her mental health and encourages people to let someone know if they are struggling:

*"There's no reason to suffer in silence...There's so many of us out there that are experiencing the same thing. You're definitely not alone."*

With the help of therapists and support from her family, she found ways to deal with her depression. Some techniques she found helpful were journaling and having small daily goals. Lindsey would spend a few minutes of the day simply writing down how she felt in a notebook and would try to focus on small everyday wins to keep her motivated.

Lindsey's kindness and compassion extend far beyond the ski slopes. She founded the Lindsey Vonn Foundation to support and empower girls. She also collaborates with the After-School All-Stars program, assisting children from low-income or less-supported family backgrounds. She also supports women pursuing athletic excellence by providing scholarships and is actively involved in eleven charitable organizations.

Lindsey's list of achievements is long and impressive, but her impact goes much deeper. Her legacy isn't just in the medals or the records but in the powerful message she embodies. Lindsey's life shows us that winning isn't just about crossing the finish line first; it's about getting back up whenever you're knocked down. It's about showing the kind of grit that keeps you moving forward even when things get tough. In Lindsey's words: *"When you fall, get right back up."*

### *Instances of Grit & Grace:*

### *Grit:*

- Competing in the 2006 Olympics, despite suffering a serious crash in practice runs. Despite the bruises and pain, Lindsey was back on the slopes two days later.
- Repeatedly pushing through painful rehabilitations to return to skiing after injuries, including fractures, torn ligaments, and severe bruising.

*Grace:*

- Her gratitude at having the opportunity to pursue her passion for skiing, which bought her joy for so many years
- The way she responded to hurtful media comments. In some cases, she chose not to respond at all, showing that sometimes silence can send a very powerful message. When she felt a response was necessary, she ensured it was polite and respectful, reinforcing the idea that being kind is far more effective than being harsh.
- Her work off the ski slopes – supporting and empowering girls through the Lindsey Vonn Foundation and her other extensive charity work.

*Key Life Lessons:*

- **Find Role Models to Inspire You:** Lindsey's meeting with her hero, Picabo Street, set her on the path to Olympic greatness, showing the powerful impact a role model can have in shaping our dreams and ambitions.
- **Be Resilient:** Despite multiple injuries and setbacks, Lindsey always found the strength to get back up and continue pursuing her dreams.
- **Be Grateful for What You Have**: Whenever she was injured, Lindsey would try to remain positive and feel grateful for having a body that could heal and recover. When times are tough, and things don't work out as we hope, remaining grateful and positive can help us move forward and keep working towards our dreams.
- **It's Okay Not to Feel Okay Sometimes:** Everyone feels down or upset occasionally – it's a normal part of being human, not a sign of weakness. Sharing your feelings with someone you trust can really help. Simple actions like writing in a journal or celebrating small wins and achievements can also make a big difference.

Lindsey Vonn's tale teaches us so much about resilience, keeping at it, and turning tough times into big wins. As we think about her adventures, it's a nudge to remember that pushing through hard times is something we can all do, not just in sports but when faced with any challenge life throws our way.

Now, we move from the ski slopes to the ice rink. Join us as we skate into the story of an ice hockey legend who has broken barriers, shattered records, and paved the way for future generations of female hockey players.

# 4

# HAYLEY WICKENHEISER

"People would say, "Girls don't play hockey. Girls don't skate." I would say, "Watch this." "

Hayley Wickenheiser

This is the story of Hayley Wickenheiser, whose journey from a small-town girl playing hockey on a frozen backyard rink to becoming one of the greatest female hockey players of all time showcases the incredible power of persistence and grit. Her story demonstrates that regardless of the challenges we face, determination and hard work can lead to remarkable success. Many believe she is the greatest female ice hockey player ever. Now, let's see what you think. Get ready to skate through the obstacles of gender barriers to discover what it takes to reach the top in women's ice hockey.

Hayley Wickenheiser's story begins in a small town in Canada, where it wasn't common for girls to play hockey. However, her parents believed wholeheartedly that a girl could do anything a boy could do. Hayley was always encouraged to dream big and had two very different goals growing up: to play for the Edmonton Oilers and to attend Harvard Medical School. These dreams may have seemed far-fetched to some, but not to Hayley or her supportive family.

Hayley's parents, both teachers, encouraged their kids to be independent and always supported their choices. While they never pushed Hayley or her siblings into a particular activity, they made sure they stayed active. In their close-knit community, life often revolved around the rink, and Hayley thrived in this environment. Winters were filled with hockey games, while summers shifted to softball—a sport she also played at a high level.

Hayley and her father often watched hockey games together, particularly those featuring her favorite team, the Edmonton Oilers. Captivated by the moves of National Hockey League (NHL) stars, Hayley would lace up her skates and head to the backyard rink, practicing tirelessly to mimic her heroes, further honing her skills.

All the kids in the neighborhood played together on and off the ice rink. Despite being the only girl, Hayley was accepted as an important member of the hockey team. With her parents and coaches recognizing her talent and supporting her every step of the way, both her skills and love for hockey grew stronger.

However, Hayley's journey into the world of competitive hockey wasn't a smooth glide across the ice. As her skills sharpened and she started playing at more advanced levels, she faced waves of discrimination that tested her resolve. Imagine being exceptional at something you love but constantly having to prove you deserve to be there. That was Hayley's reality.

One year, Hayley wanted to join a hockey camp to improve her skills, but it was an all-boys camp. The organizers eventually let her participate, but there was a catch—she had to sleep in a closet. Yes, you read that right, a tiny, cramped closet! However, Hayley wasn't alone in this struggle; her younger brother was at the camp, too. He felt sorry for her and willingly squeezed into the closet with her each night, providing some much-needed support.

With Hayley's growing hockey skills and increased competitive play, her commitment only deepened. Yet, the challenges she faced also increased, especially the doubts about her abilities, simply because she was a girl in a male-dominated sport.

By this time, Hayley and her family had moved to Calgary, and Hayley was playing in competitive leagues with boys, often as the only girl on the team. She frequently felt isolated and alone, having to change by herself in boiler rooms or bathroom stalls. She sometimes had things thrown at her and faced harassment from parents who didn't think she should take a boy's place on the team. To blend in and avoid abuse, she cut her hair short and tried to look like a boy. It's hard to believe what Hayley had to endure, but she saw the discrimination as a challenge she had to face to play the sport she loved.

Fortunately, Hayley had a strong support system—her family and coaches who truly believed in her abilities. Whenever she faced tough times, they reminded her of her talent and potential. Even so, her parents saw how hard it was for her and often asked her if she wanted to quit, wanting to protect her from the harassment she faced. However, Hayley refused to take the criticism to heart. Instead of letting negative comments bring her down, she adopted an "I'll prove you wrong" mentality and worked even harder. She loved playing hockey too much to stop, and on the ice, she felt safe. No one could criticize or bully her there. Every time she laced up her skates, she proved to herself and everyone else that she had a right to play.

In 1991, at just 12 years old, Hayley played in her first major tournament for Alberta in the Canada Winter Games. Despite being the youngest and shortest player, she stunned everyone watching with her skills and talent. Hayley scored three goals and shot the game-winning goal in the final. Alberta won the gold medal, and Hayley was named the team's MVP.

Fast forward three years, fifteen-year-old Hayley found herself on the international stage at the International Ice Hockey Federation (IIHF) Women's World Hockey Championship, representing Team Canada. She was the youngest player on the team and 20 years younger than her captain! Hayley made a huge impact, playing in three games and providing a crucial assist to help Canada win the gold medal.

In 1998, Hayley was chosen to join Team Canada for the Winter Olympics. It should have been a dream come true, but it proved to be a bittersweet experience. Canada lost to the USA in the final, leaving Hayley devastated. The defeat was tough to accept, but Hayley used it as fuel rather than letting it crush her spirit. Determined never to feel that way again, Hayley pushed herself to work harder, train longer, and stay even more focused on her goals.

By the time the next Winter Olympics rolled around in Salt Lake City in 2002, Hayley was ready. And this time, everything came together perfectly. Canada won the gold medal, and Hayley was instrumental in their victory, scoring one of the winning goals in the final. She emerged as one of the tournament's top scorers with seven goals and three assists. Her journey from disappointment to triumph is a powerful reminder that setbacks can be stepping stones to success if we learn from them and work hard to improve.

Back in Canada, Hayley was a standout player in the Canadian Women's Hockey League (CWHL), representing teams including

Alberta, the Edmonton Chimos, and the Calgary Oval X-Treme and securing multiple championships and honors.

In 2003, Hayley Wickenheiser made a bold and brave decision: she moved to Finland to join a professional men's hockey team, becoming the first woman to play professional men's hockey in a position other than goalie. This move took her far out of her comfort zone. Not only was she in a new country where she didn't speak the language, but she was also the only woman on the team.

From day one, she faced intense media scrutiny. Reporters were eager to catch any mistakes or signs that she might not be up to the challenge of playing in the men's league. The pressure was immense, especially for someone so far from home. During one of her early games, she took a stick to the face, breaking her nose. With all eyes on her and feeling isolated, Hayley was close to breaking point. But she refused to let her teammates, or the media see her cry. Hayley was determined to keep going, even when everything seemed against her.

A couple of nights later, Hayley made hockey history by becoming the first woman to score a goal in a men's professional league. Often, when facing our hardest moments, great things are just around the corner. Hayley's first goal was proof that hard work and grit do pay off, even when the odds seem stacked against you.

Despite her success, Hayley's struggles were far from over. As the only girl playing professional men's hockey, she always faced challenges finding a place to change before and after games. For home games, she would change in a referee's room by herself and then walk down the hall to join her teammates. Though it felt a bit lonely, it was manageable. However, away matches were a different story. She recalls a trip to Northern Finland for a game where the coach didn't think girls should play hockey. Instead of providing a suitable changing room, the coach told her to change with the team's cheerleaders. This attempt to undermine her only strengthened Hayley's resolve. That night, her team won, and she was named player of the match.

Hayley returned to play women's hockey in Canada in 2004. Over the next eight years, she continued to break barriers and impress the world with her incredible hockey skills, winning numerous medals and awards.

In 2012, Hayley injured her foot during practice. The doctors didn't think it was serious, so she took a short break to recover and was soon back on the ice, training intensively for the 2014 Olympics. However, just before the Sochi Olympics, she discovered that what she had believed to be a sprain was actually a fracture. Hayley refused to pull out: She pushed through the pain, helping lead Canada to a dramatic overtime gold medal win over the USA.

By playing on her injured foot, Hayley caused further damage. The first set of operations seemed successful, but she re-injured her foot and needed more surgery. As she listened to the doctors, only one thing went through her mind: *Will I ever play hockey again?* Extensive rehabilitation followed the second surgery, but Hayley's determination to return to the ice never wavered.

Hayley returned to the ice in 2016 and played professional hockey for two more seasons. She retired from professional hockey in 2017, wanting to spend more time with her son and pursue other dreams. She enrolled in medical school, determined to fulfill her second childhood dream. As if that wasn't enough, she continues to be deeply involved in the hockey world. She founded WickFest, an annual festival championing girls' and women's hockey, which brings together female players from around the world for a series of games and workshops to inspire and develop their skills. Hayley is also assistant director of player development for the Toronto Maple Leafs and is the first woman to hold this position.

Hayley Wickenheiser is widely considered the greatest female hockey player of all time. She won seven gold medals and six silver medals with Team Canada at the IIHF Women's World Hockey Championships and four gold medals and one silver medal at the Olympic Winter Games. Hayley is Canada's all-time leader in international goals (168), assists (211), and points (379). She has been recognized as one of the toughest women in sports, one of the top 50 most powerful women in Canada, and one of the top 100 most influential people in hockey. What makes Hayley's story so inspiring isn't just her accolades and records. It's the sheer grit and perseverance she showed in the face of adversity.

*Instances of Grit and Grace:*

*Grit:*

- Sleeping in a closet so she could participate in an all-boys hockey camp.
- Fighting for her place on the ice despite the discrimination and harsh criticism she faced as a girl competing in a male-dominated sport.
- Her determination to keep playing despite the media scrutiny and loneliness she felt playing in a men's league in Finland.
- Her unwavering dedication to recover from her foot surgery so she could lace up her skates and play competitively again.

*Grace*

- The dignified way she dealt with the discrimination and hurtful comments she faced for being a girl wanting to play a predominantly male sport – choosing to let her hockey skills do the talking.
- Championing a drive for personal protective equipment for front-line healthcare workers during the Covid-19 pandemic.
- Her commitment to giving back to the community through her charity work and inspiring and empowering young female hockey players through WickFest.

*Key Life Lessons:*

- **Be Willing to Step Out of Your Comfort Zone**: There are so many times when Hayley had to step out of her comfort zone, from playing with boys while growing up, competing with

older women, to joining a men's professional hockey team in a country thousands of miles from home. Taking on big, scary challenges can be incredibly hard, but they're the best way to grow. These experiences, though tough in the moment, help us become stronger and more resilient.
- **Be Ready to Face Setbacks:** Like Hayley's broken nose and injured foot, challenges will come, and they may knock you down. The key is to get back up and keep pushing forward.
- **Use Adversity and Criticism as Fuel:** When situations seem unfair, like Hayley being told to change with the cheerleaders, use that frustration to drive you to work harder and prove the doubters wrong.

For many, Hayley's greatest impact is how she has transformed the game for girls. When she was invited to join the Hockey Hall of Fame, she spoke of her vision for the future, hoping that girls:

*"If they decide to play hockey, they can walk into a hockey rink anywhere in Canada with a hockey bag and hockey stick over the shoulder and nobody's going to look at you twice, they won't have to cut their hair short and run into the bathroom and try to look like a boy like I had to do to blend in. The road is just a little bit easier."*

What powerful words and such an incredible legacy.

Next up, we will be hitting the basketball court and shooting for success. See you there!

## 5

# TAMIKA CATCHINGS

"The highs and lows I experienced during my second year, my second grade ... gave me that drive, the drive to succeed."

Tamika Catchings

We're now embarking on a journey with Tamika Catchings, following her from the difficult days of feeling left out as a child to becoming one of the greatest female basketball players ever. Tamika's story is about overcoming adversity and having the courage to find your voice.

Tamika Catchings was born into a basketball-loving family. Her father, Harvey Catchings, was a famous National Basketball Association (NBA) player in the 70s and 80s. Growing up, Tamika's family moved frequently, but basketball was a constant in her life. Tamika was diagnosed with hearing loss at just three years old, which meant she had to wear large hearing aids and made communication challenging.

In second grade, after her family returned to Texas following a year in Italy, Tamika first realized she was different. She was the tallest girl in her class, wore bulky hearing aids, had trouble hearing, and spoke differently from her classmates. Tamika was desperate to blend in, feel ordinary, and be like the other girls. But every day at school, her peers made fun of her and reminded her of her differences. Some days, she walked home with tears streaming down her face, longing to be invisible so the teasing would stop. When she arrived home, Tamika would plead with her mom not to make her go back to school.

One day, after relentless teasing, Tamika had had enough. Walking home from school, she passed a field filled with long grass. In a moment of desperation, she took out her hearing aids and threw them as far as she could, hoping that without them, she would finally be accepted at school and left alone.

Later that evening, when her mom picked her up from softball practice, she noticed Tamika wasn't wearing her aids. Tamika pretended she didn't know where she had lost them. Together, they searched the softball field, the school, and the route to and from school but couldn't find them. Tamika never admitted where they were. Her parents explained that they couldn't afford another set, and Tamika would have to learn to live without them.

Tamika did just that. In class, she would sit right up front, reading chapters before lessons to stay ahead. She learned to lip-read so she could understand what her teachers said and stayed behind after class to ask questions about anything she didn't catch. Life became a little bit easier for Tamika. The other kids could no longer tease her about her big hearing aids, and she could no longer hear all their mean comments.

Tamika loved sports. At first, she played soccer and softball, but basketball truly lit a fire in her heart. Coached by her dad, she played whenever she could, and often practiced in the yard with her sister. Both girls were very competitive, and their games sometimes led to fierce arguments. When this happened, their dad would take the ball away. While her sister retreated to her bedroom, Tamika stayed outside, practicing her skills without a ball.

Picking up basketball was more than just a hobby—it became Tamika's sanctuary.

*"Whenever I got mad, I would play basketball; whenever I was happy, I would play basketball. Anything I was feeling, I'd play basketball."*

In seventh grade, she made a bold decision and excitedly wrote it on a piece of paper: she was going to play in the NBA one day. She rushed to tell her brother and sister, then ran downstairs to share her goal with her parents. Her parents smiled and said, *"If anyone can do it, you can."* She ran back upstairs and stuck the piece of paper up in her bathroom. Every morning, as she brushed her teeth, she thought about her goal, determined to make her dream a reality.

Tamika's dedication to practicing and improving her skills started to show, and she soon became one of the top basketball players in school. Her life became a little easier. Nobody made fun of her on the court; everyone wanted her on their team. People started to see her for the athlete she was, not just the girl who couldn't hear well.

At 15, Tamika became the youngest Miss Illinois Basketball. She and her sister Tauja were driving forces on the school basketball team.

Tamika's competitive nature made winning important, but having fun with her teammates mattered just as much. Finally, Tamika felt accepted and had friends to hang out with.

However, just as Tamika was starting to feel happier and more settled at school, her parents announced they were getting divorced. Tamika's dad planned to stay in Chicago with Tauja so she could finish her senior year at high school. Tamika moved with her mother to Texas to be closer to her mom's family.

The change was tough for Tamika. She had to start at a new school and deal with her hearing disability without the support of her brother and sister. During the first few months, Tamika often felt very alone, adjusting to life without her siblings close by and looking to make new friends. She found herself once again yearning to fit in and be accepted. But amidst all the upheaval, Tamika found refuge in basketball. The sport was a place where she felt normal, even when everything around her seemed incredibly different.

Fast forward a year: Tamika is now in her senior year. The crowd at Duncanville High watched in awe as Tamika achieved something no other player in history had ever done. She recorded a quintuple-double, with double digits in all five categories in one game: 25 points, 18 rebounds, 11 assists, 10 steals, and 10 blocked shots. Her coaches, teammates, and spectators were amazed by her performance, realizing they were witnessing a future basketball sensation in action. That year, Tamika also helped her school secure the Texas Championship title, and she was awarded the Naismith Trophy as the National Girls' High School Player of the Year.

Winning the Naismith Award led to many university scholarship offers. She chose to accept a scholarship to play basketball at the University of Tennessee (UT) under the legendary coach Pat Summitt. Under Coach Summitt's mentorship, Tamika flourished. She honed her skills, developed her leadership qualities, and became a critical player in the Lady Volunteers (Lady Vols). In her first season, she set a Tennessee freshman record by averaging 18.2 points per game and played a crucial role in helping Tennessee win the 1998 National Collegiate Athletics Association (NCAA) tournament, scoring a team-high 27 points. Although many believed Catchings deserved the MVP award for that game, it went to another teammate. Nonetheless, she received other honors, including the Naismith National Freshman of the Year award and the US Basketball Writers Association Freshman of the Year award. Additionally, she was named to the Kodak All-American team, becoming only the fourth freshman to achieve this recognition.

While at college in Tennessee, Tamika's coaches encouraged her to reconsider wearing hearing aids and start speech therapy. They helped her see that her story could inspire thousands, maybe even millions, of people. With their support, Tamika began to realize the power of her story and the positive influence it could have on others. She finally accepted her hearing loss and started wearing hearing aids again for the first time since third grade.

The Women's National Basketball Association (WNBA) was created while Tamika was at university, making her dreams of playing professional basketball even more realistic. However, in her last year at university, Tamika tore her ACL, a devastating injury that prevented her from playing for an entire season. Frustrated and worried that no WNBA team would want her, she was overjoyed when she was chosen 3rd in the draft. Indiana Fever took a chance on her, knowing she couldn't make an immediate impact but believing in her potential. Tamika credits her Christian faith with helping her through this difficult time.

Indiana Fever's faith in Tamika paid off enormously. After a frustrating year sitting on the sidelines, Tamika stunned the basketball world with her skills and energy, winning the Rookie of the Year award. She had used her time on the sidelines wisely, watching and learning – determined to come back better and stronger.

Tamika played with the Indiana Fever for her entire WNBA career and became the heart and soul of the team. Her commitment and drive inspired her teammates, motivating them to push their boundaries and strive for greatness. She grew into a respected leader, admired not only for her talent but also for her unwavering spirit and resilience.

For Tamika Catchings, being part of a team was one of the most rewarding experiences. After struggling to fit in as a child, she found a sense of belonging on the basketball court. Tamika loved cheering on her teammates, enthusiastically celebrating their efforts and achievements. No matter how stellar her performance, Tamika always credited her teammates, focusing on the importance of the team's victory over her personal achievements. She understood that being a great teammate meant supporting each other on and off the court. Her positive attitude and encouragement inspired her teammates to give their best, making her not just a star player but also a beloved and respected team member.

Over the years, Tamika kept pushing boundaries, shattering records, and collecting awards. However, one goal remained just out of reach: winning the WNBA Championship. In 2009, the Indiana Fever came close, competing in their first-ever WNBA Finals against the Phoenix Mercury. The Fever lost the opening game in overtime but bounced back to win the next two games in Indianapolis, putting them ahead 2-1 in the series and just one win away from the Championship. However, they lost the next game, making the final game decisive. The Championship came down to free throws, and Phoenix's perfect shooting in the final minute dashed Indiana Fever's hopes of securing the WNBA title. Tamika and the team were devastated; they had come so close.

However, Tamika was determined to keep trying, never losing faith that they would win the Championship one day.

In 2012, Tamika's dream came true when the Indiana Fever secured their first-ever WNBA Championship. Despite battling injuries all season and missing key players in the Finals, the team's unwavering determination and refusal to give up hope led them to victory.

Tamika's dedication and hard work have made her one of the greatest players in basketball history. She has collected many awards, including being an 11-time WNBA All-Star and a 12-time All-WNBA player.

She was named Defensive Player of the Year five times, won 2 MVP awards, was voted in the WNBA's Top 15 Players of All Time by fans, and secured a place in the Basketball Hall of Fame. She was also an invaluable member of the US basketball team, helping them win four Olympic gold medals and two World Championship golds.

Tamika retired in 2016 with big dreams to help others and inspire the next generation. She set up the "Catch the Stars Foundation," which aims to empower youth by providing fitness, literacy, and mentoring programs.

Tamika also gives motivational speeches, captivating audiences with her story and encouraging others to embrace their uniqueness and believe in themselves. For someone who hardly spoke as a child due to hearing challenges, standing in front of crowds and speaking confidently is nothing short of remarkable.

### *Instances of Grit and Grace:*

### *Grit:*

- Developing effective strategies to keep up with her studies without her hearing aids.
- Her refusal to let her hearing loss hinder her dreams of becoming a basketball legend – turning it into her 'superpower' by becoming very observant on the court and developing an incredible ability to predict plays before they happened.
- Her determination to win the WNBA championship with the Indiana Fever. It took 12 seasons, filled with setbacks and near-misses. But her unwavering commitment and hard work finally led her team to victory in 2012.
- Finding her voice – working with speech therapists at UT and countless hours of practicing to become a confident public speaker.

*Grace*

- In some of her matches at school, she received undeserved fouls for being one of the only girls of color on the team. She responded with dignity, refusing to lose her composure or argue with officials.
- Tamika was a beloved and respected team member. She understood that being a great teammate meant cheering for and supporting each other on and off the court.
- Her work after retiring from basketball – empowering youth through her "Catch the Stars Foundation".
- A core message in her motivational speeches - 'Lead with Love.'

*Key Life Lessons:*

- **Embrace Your Uniqueness:** Like Tamika, who turned her hearing loss into a strength, you can embrace what makes you unique. Her journey shows that being different can be your greatest asset, helping you stand out and achieve greatness.
- **There is no "I" in "Team:"** Tamika valued her teammates and celebrated their successes as much as her own. Her story teaches us that success and happiness come from working together and supporting one another.
- **Sport and Other Hobbies Can Help You Through Tough Times**: Tamika turned to basketball during her difficult school years, using the sport as a way to escape and feel happier.
- **You Can Overcome Your Weaknesses**: Tamika Catchings struggled with confidence in speaking as a child due to hearing loss. Despite this, she didn't let her weakness define her and went on to become a motivational speaker, inspiring others with her story and showing that with time and effort, weaknesses can be overcome.

Tamika Catchings became a role model not just for her incredible basketball skills but for never letting obstacles like her hearing loss, her parents' divorce, or injuries stop her from achieving her dreams. Let it be a reminder that we all have the power to turn our dreams into reality, and sometimes, the things that set us apart are the very things that make us extraordinary.

Our next chapter involves a trip to Sweden to meet a golfing legend – another incredible girl who swung her way to stardom in a sport mostly played by men.

# 6

# ANNIKA SÖRENSTAM

"I push myself to be the best I can be. I don't worry about what other people are doing, and I don't think about things I can't control."

Annika Sörenstam

Annika Sorenstam's journey from a quiet, shy girl who hated being the center of attention to becoming a golf icon is nothing short of amazing. It's the story of a girl who, from the snowy landscapes of Sweden to the lush greens around the globe, faced her fears and persevered through challenges, ultimately transforming women's golf and paving the way for future generations.

Annika was born on October 9, 1970, in Bro, a small town near Stockholm, Sweden. Growing up in a sports-loving family, she initially showed more interest in tennis and skiing than in golf and excelled at both. Her father, a keen golfer, introduced Annika and her younger sister, Charlotta, to the game. As their love for golf grew, he gave them a set of clubs to share. To prevent arguments between the sisters, Annika was given the odd-numbered clubs, while her sister used the even-numbered ones. What started as a fun family activity soon became a passion for Annika as she discovered the joys and challenges of the game.

When Annika was 15 years old, she and Charlotta stepped into the exciting world of big-time golf at a major tournament in Stockholm. The event was part of the prestigious European Tour, known for hosting Europe's biggest men's golf competitions. Eager to get close to the action, the sisters volunteered as "golf caddies", ready to carry the heavy golf bags for the professional players. All the boys who volunteered were picked first - Annika, Charlotta, and another girl were last chosen. They refused to let the outdated views that golf is a man's game dampen their enthusiasm and love for the sport.

Annika was not a young golf prodigy who dominated from the start. Instead, she was a diligent student of the game, always eager to learn and improve. However, initially, her dedication to practicing wavered. One particularly cold and rainy day, she called her father to pick her up early from training. As they drove away, she noticed some friends still out on the course, practicing in the rain. Her dad turned to her and said, *"Annika, there are no shortcuts."* That moment was a turning point for Annika. She realized that to achieve her goals, she had to fully commit. She dedicated countless hours to practice and made time to watch her idols playing – mostly male players since women's golf was rarely televised. She experimented with their techniques, always looking for ways to improve her game.

At first, Annika spent most of her time practicing and perfecting her favorite shots, the ones she was best at. But soon enough, she realized that to be the best, she would also need to work on her weaker shots, so she started working hard on turning her weaknesses into strengths. This shift in mindset—to balance working on both strengths and areas needing improvement—is a game-changer no matter what field you're in.

All the while, Annika was fighting another battle: she was desperately shy. Her father encouraged her to focus on her game and let her clubs 'do the talking,' but being in the spotlight felt daunting. During her early competitions, Annika often played poorly toward the end to avoid winning, as victory meant giving a speech. The thought of public speaking scared her more than any competitor on the course. She remembers feeling relieved she wouldn't have to speak in front of others but also disappointed knowing she hadn't played her best. Anyone shy or nervous about speaking in public will relate to Annika's comment: *"I really just wanted to take the trophy and run away, but it just doesn't work like that."*

When her father realized what Annika was doing, he spoke to the tournament organizers, and they agreed that the top 3 finishers should give a short speech. Annika realized she would need to face her fear if she really wanted to become a great golfer.

*"I realized then that I had to face my fears. I wanted to be a good player, but when you have things in your way, it blocks your success."*

Her father gave her a couple of great tips for public speaking: he suggested she talk about her love for golf and how she had played that day, topics he knew she'd feel more comfortable discussing. He also encouraged her to practice her speech beforehand, so it would feel easier and less daunting.

As Annika's golf skills improved, so did her competitive spirit. After every tournament, she would thoroughly review her performance to identify both her strengths and areas for improvement. This smart way of analyzing her play became key to her success.

Annika had a successful amateur career before turning professional. She competed in the Espirito Santo Trophy in 1990 and 1992, clinching the individual title in 1992. During 1990-91, she won three tournaments on the Swedish Golf Tour and was a key player on the Swedish National Team from 1987 to 1992. Annika continued to excel when she moved to the United States to play college golf at the University of Arizona. There, she won seven collegiate events, including the 1991 NCAA Division I Individual Championship during her freshman year.

Turning professional in 1992, Annika's early years were a mix of successes and learning opportunities. She didn't secure a win immediately but remained determined, continually fine-tuning her skills and believing in her abilities. Her dedication paid off in 1995 when she clinched her first major title at the US Women's Open, staging a remarkable comeback from five shots behind. This victory not only showcased her impressive golfing skills but also her mental resilience, firmly establishing her presence in the world of women's golf.

Annika went from strength to strength for the next few years, winning multiple prestigious tournaments, including the 1995 Australian Ladies Masters and a second US Women's Open title in 1996. She became the first non-American to win the Vare Trophy, achieving this honor in 1995 and 1996. Additionally, she won the Rolex Player of the Year award in 1995, 1997, and 1998.

Annika faced a challenging time in 1999-2000; having achieved so many of her goals, she lost focus and found herself slipping from the top spot she had worked so hard to reach. Annika knew she needed to rethink her strategy. She thoroughly reviewed her recent performances and statistics, pinpointing areas where she could improve. She then set herself a challenging goal – to be no. 1 in all aspects of her game. Annika worked with coaches to improve her weaker areas and revamped her fitness regimen to enhance her strength and stamina. Her commitment paid off. By 2001, she had reclaimed the Ladies Professional Golf Association (LPGA) Player of the Year title and won eight LPGA tournaments. That same year, she set another record – becoming the first (and only) female golfer to score a 59 in a Tour competition.

Annika Sörenstam's story would be incomplete without highlighting a defining moment in 2003—her participation in the Colonial, a men's Professional Golf Association (PGA) tournament. By accepting this invitation, she became the first woman since 1945 to compete in a men's professional golf tournament. The choice to play was loaded with challenges, including significant pressure, criticism, and relentless media attention. Many in the golf community, particularly men, criticized her participation, doubting her skills and clinging to the old-fashioned notion that golf was a men's sport.

However, some men, including US golf commentator David Faherty, supported Annika's brave decision. With a daughter of his own, he believed that, regardless of her score at the end of the tournament, her participation sent an important, inspiring message to young girls: *"Simply for her to show that she has the courage to do this is fantastic. The most important message is that you have to try."*

Annika refused to listen to the criticism, recognizing the opportunity as a once-in-a-lifetime chance to challenge herself and break through another barrier.

Annika stepped onto the course, battling nerves and the weight of expectation; she says she was so nervous that she couldn't speak as she walked to the first hole. She chose to focus on what she does best – playing golf, taking one shot at a time, and trying to block out the enormity and significance of the event.

The tournament was more than a personal challenge; it was a symbolic moment for women in sports. Parents drove thousands of miles just so their daughters could witness a woman competing on equal footing with men, demonstrating that gender should not define one's aspirations or abilities.

Though Annika did not win, she outperformed some of the men who participated. More importantly, her participation gave her newfound confidence and profoundly impacted the sports world, inspiring a generation to dream big.

After years of competing at the highest level, Annika reached a point where her heart was no longer in the game. She had other passions and dreams to explore beyond the golf course. Recognizing her waning motivation, she made the bold decision to retire while still at the top of her game, following her triumph at an LPGA tournament in May 2008. Today, Annika Sörenstam is much more than a retired golfer. She is a role model, an entrepreneur, and an advocate for women in sports. Through her foundation, she continues to inspire and empower young girls to pursue their dreams in golf and life. She also designs golf courses and still receives criticism from some men who say her courses are too easy!

Throughout her career, Annika won 72 LPGA tournaments, 10 major titles, and 8 Player of the Year awards. She is the only LPGA Tour player to score a 59 and has earned a place in the LPGA Hall of Fame. Her legacy goes beyond these awards; her journey teaches us about the importance of passion, perseverance, and having the courage to face our fears.

*Instances of Grit and Grace:*

*Grit:*

- The countless hours spent perfecting her shots, the determination not only to improve on her good shots but also to master her weaker shots.
- Stepping up to speak in front of crowds despite her fears of public speaking.
- Refusing to let the negativity and criticism she faced stop her from chasing her dreams and breaking barriers.
- Her comeback after losing focus in 1999-2000, analyzing every aspect of her game and addressing her weaknesses to ensure a triumphant return.

*Grace:*

- Remaining professional and poised despite the intense scrutiny and media pressure when she played in a men's tournament – choosing to focus on showcasing her skills on the golf course.
- Annika is known for being friendly and respectful with colleagues and competitors.
- Her work with the Annika Foundation inspires and encourages girls to believe in their dreams, both in golf and in other aspects of life.

*Key Life Lessons:*

- **Be Willing to Face Your Fears:** Annika was shy and scared of speaking in public, but she pushed through her fears, realizing it was the key to achieving her true potential.
- **Have the Courage to Try:** Annika felt nervous when participating in the men's PGA tournament. We grow and improve by trying new things and pushing ourselves out of our comfort zones. When something feels scary, remember Annika's words: *"If you want to get better at something, if you want to test yourself, you have to have the courage to say yes."*
- **Work on Your Weaknesses:** By working on her weaknesses, Annika became the golfing legend she is today. It shows that success comes not just from what you're good at but from your willingness to tackle what you're not.
- **Success Takes Time**: Annika spent countless hours refining the weaker parts of her game before clinching major victories. Remember her father's words: *"There are no shortcuts to success."*
- **Take One Step at a Time** – When competition nerves set in, Annika concentrated on what she could control – her next shot. When a situation feels overwhelming, focusing on the next small step you need to take, rather than thinking about a

daunting end goal can make things feel more manageable and ensure you keep making progress towards your goals.

For Annika, success was never about the spotlight. What truly mattered was challenging herself to see how good she could be. Her story shows that to truly excel, you must step out of your comfort zone, take on challenges that scare you, and find the strength to keep going amidst criticism. Annika's journey isn't just one of a golfer among men; it reaches further. It reminds us that boundaries, whether they're about gender roles or our own inner fears, can be overcome.

Up next, get ready to leap into the world of gymnastics to meet a girl whose dazzling flips and spins have captivated audiences worldwide. Join us as we explore how she rose to become one of the greatest gymnasts of all time.

# 7

# SIMONE BILES

"I'd rather regret the risks that didn't work out than the chances I didn't take at all."

Simone Biles

Flipping and soaring through the air, Simone Biles has inspired and wowed the world with her strength, elegance, and grace. From her challenging beginnings in foster care to dazzling on the Olympic stage, Simone's story is one of courage, determination, and unstoppable spirit. Join us on an adventure about so much more than winning trophies and medals. Through her actions and words, Simone reminds us that when times get tough and life feels overwhelming, it's ok to take a break.

Simone Biles was born on March 14, 1997, in Columbus, Ohio, one of four children. Her early life was not easy. Her father left when she was just a baby, and her mother struggled with addiction issues. When she was only three years old, Simone and her siblings were placed into foster care. Over the next two years, the children moved from one home to another, never quite knowing how long they would stay in each place. This was a hard, confusing, and scary time for Simone.

But Simone's life took a positive turn when her grandparents, Ron and Nellie Biles, adopted her and her younger sister, Adria. With their love and support, Simone found a stable home and the encouragement she needed to thrive. Ron's sister, Harriet, adopted Simone's two older siblings.

Simone's gymnastics journey began unexpectedly during a daycare visit to a gymnastics center when she was six. She was captivated by the older girls twisting and turning in the air and began to copy their movements. Coaches at the center were amazed by her natural talent and air awareness—a skill that usually takes gymnasts years to master. Realizing Simone was a star in the making, one of the coaches sent a letter home urging Simone's grandparents to enroll her in regular gymnastics classes.

Soon after, Simone started training at Bannon's Gymnastix and rapidly became a star student. Simone devoted countless hours to learning and perfecting her techniques, developing a deep passion and love for training. According to her grandmother, she never missed practice. Even when she didn't feel well, she insisted on attending her sessions. With the help of dedicated coaches, she honed her skills. Her knack for flipping and tumbling soon became evident, and it wasn't long before she started winning competitions.

At the age of 14, Simone began competing in elite-level competitions. In her first competition, the US Classic in Houston, she came first in the vault and balance beam events and placed third all-around. To dedicate more time to her training, she started homeschooling to help balance her education with her growing gymnastics career.

In 2013, Simone won her first national all-around title at the USA Gymnastics National Championships. Her performances were nothing short of breathtaking, showcasing her extraordinary talent and unique style. She became known for her powerful routines, explosive energy, and innovative skills, leaving audiences and judges in awe. That year, Simone made history as the first African American to win the all-around title at the World Championships. She also secured the gold medal in the floor exercise. This was just the beginning of her incredible journey.

In 2016, Simone Biles made her Olympic debut at the Rio de Janeiro Games, stunning the world with her unmatched athleticism and groundbreaking routines. Her performances were truly spectacular, earning her four gold medals and one bronze. Simone's dominance in the all-around, vault, and floor events was unparalleled, making her the first female gymnast in over 30 years to win four gold medals at a single Olympic Games. Her infectious smile and unshakeable confidence made her a fan favorite and an inspiration to young gymnasts worldwide.

By the end of 2019, Simone had won 30 medals at the World Championships and Olympics – 23 of them gold. Four gymnastics moves had also been named after her – 2 floor, 1 beam, and 1 vault. In gymnastics, a move is named after an athlete if they are the first to execute it successfully and have the skill officially recognized at a major international competition.

However, Simone's journey wasn't without its challenges. Along with the physical demands of gymnastics, she faced immense pressure and expectations from the media and the public. In a sport that focuses heavily on appearance and involves body-hugging leotards, Simone faced criticism for her strong, muscular build. On one occasion, a coach even called her fat, causing Simone to walk out of the training session and break down in tears when she was alone. After a pep talk from another coach, Simone resumed her training, determined not to let the hurtful comments affect her. She credits her teammate Aly Raisman with helping her with her body confidence issues. Simone admits: *"I've learned to put on a strong front and let most of it slide... But I'd be lying if I told you that what people say about my arms, my legs, my body...of how I look like in a dress, leotard, bathing suit, or even in casual pants hasn't gotten me down at times."*

Shockingly, some people failed to recognize that these very muscles contributed to her record-breaking performances.

Over time, Simone has learned to ignore the criticism and embrace her beauty – something we should all try to do. Simone has become a role model for young African American gymnasts and athletes, showing that success is not determined by the color of your skin:

*"I wanted them to know that following your dreams—not just in gymnastics, but in everything—shouldn't have anything to do with the color of your skin. It should only be about finding the discipline and the courage to do the hard work."*

Simone has worked with beauty brands and appeared in major advertisements to challenge unrealistic beauty standards and encourage self-acceptance. In a campaign for the beauty brand SK-II, her picture features alongside the empowering words: *"It doesn't matter what other people say, it's my body, and it does incredible things."*

Simone faced another challenge in September 2016 when her medical records were leaked, revealing that she was taking medication for ADHD. She was accused of using illegal substances to enhance her performance, which left her devastated. Simone courageously addressed the issue, being open about her diagnosis and working to reduce the stigma around both the condition and the need for medication. Her honesty and vulnerability inspired many others facing similar struggles.

Fast forward to Tokyo 2021—the eyes of the world were again on Simone for the postponed 2020 Olympic Games. The pressure was immense; could Simone win back-to-back Olympic medals and achieve something no one had done in over 50 years? She was the star of the games, with everyone expecting her to break records, win multiple gold medals, and secure her legacy as the greatest gymnast ever. However, early rounds showed signs of trouble: awkward landings, falling off the beam, and tears as she left the floor. Something wasn't right.

Now, let me take you to the critical day, the team final. Simone is preparing to start on the vault, staring into the bleachers. She knows she has one of the most difficult moves in gymnastics ahead of her, the Amanar, which involves two-and-a-half twists in the air.

Simone takes a deep breath and starts running. She performs a round-off and back handspring onto and off the vault. She twists and turns in midair but completes only one-and-a-half twists, landing awkwardly and lunging forward. There is stunned silence in the arena, and the commentators struggle to explain what they've just seen. Simone walks off the mat in tears, speaks to her coaching team, and then leaves the competition floor.

A little later, Simone walks back into the arena and approaches her teammates. Soon, they are all in tears. Simone tells them she is withdrawing from the team final, explaining she doesn't want to let them down or jeopardize their chance of winning a medal.

A statement later that day sent shockwaves around the world, confirming that Simone was withdrawing from the team final. In the following days, she also withdrew from the individual all-around competition, vault, uneven bars, and floor finals, choosing to prioritize her physical and mental health over medals. Simone felt an immense sense of guilt, believing she was disappointing her teammates, her country, and the thousands of fans who had supported her and therapists for supporting her through the tough times and encouraging her to keep going.

Simone returned triumphantly to competition in 2023, capturing the world's attention again with her mesmerizing skills and routines. She won her eighth all-around title at the US National Championships and placed first in the balance beam and floor events. In October 2023, Simone competed at the World Championships, winning her sixth all-around gold medal. With this title, she became the most successful female gymnast of all time at both the Olympics and World Championships. At this event, a fifth skill was named after her when she became the first woman to land a Yurchenko double pike, now known as the Biles II (Vault). At the Olympic Games in Paris, she won another 3 gold medals and one silver – once again, dazzling the world with her performances.

Simone's comeback not only reaffirmed her status as one of the greatest gymnasts of all time but showed us that true excellence includes taking care of our mental and emotional well-being.

Aside from her spectacular flips and leaps, Simone finds time to support and inspire others. She has never forgotten her roots in foster care and works with a children's charity that pairs foster kids with supportive, long-term mentors. She champions gender equality and openly shares her experiences with mental health, encouraging young people everywhere to speak up and seek help. Simone also uses her platform to urge young girls to embrace their bodies, regardless of shape or size. Through interviews, social media, and public appearances, Simone regularly speaks out against body shaming. Her message is clear: love yourself as you are and recognize your body for the amazing things it can do, not just how it looks.

journey. It was later revealed that Simone was suffering from the "twisties", a condition where the mind and body don't work together, causing the brain to lose track of the body's position in the air. This can be extremely dangerous, especially during high-risk flips and twists.

Simone participated in the beam final, performing a less complicated routine than initially planned. She wanted to compete in at least one event at the Olympics, but this time, she was doing it for herself, not worrying about winning a medal. Simone took home the bronze and watched the remaining events from the stands, supporting and cheering on her teammates and congratulating other competitors on their performances.

It took immense courage for Simone, one of the stars of the US Olympic team and a global gymnastics megastar, to step back from something so significant, especially with the world watching. Her decision sparked a global conversation about the importance of mental health in sports, highlighting the immense pressure athletes face and the need for greater support and understanding. While many applauded her for putting her well-being first, others unfairly labeled her a quitter.

Simone's story teaches us an invaluable lesson: prioritizing your mental well-being doesn't make you weak. Sometimes, it's okay not to be okay. It's easy to get caught up in trying to be the best and pushing yourself as hard as you can, but sometimes, knowing when to take a break and look after yourself is just as important.

For some time after Tokyo, Simone wasn't sure if she would return to competitive gymnastics. However, deep down, she felt her story wasn't finished and didn't want her incredible career to end that way.

So, after a much-needed break, Simone returned to training - but it wasn't easy. She had to work incredibly hard, not just on her strength and skills but also on her mindset. There were many moments when she felt like quitting—it was tough both physically and mentally. In the documentary *Simone Biles: Rising,* she reveals that she *"wanted to quit, like, 500,000 times."* She credits her coaches, teammates, family

*Instances of Grit and Grace*

*Grit*

- Consistently pushing the boundaries in women's gymnastics by performing exceptionally difficult moves and routines, often never previously attempted by women.
- With the eyes of the world on her following her decision to withdraw from some events at the Tokyo Olympics, Simone was determined to compete in the balance beam event.
- Her persistence in chasing her dreams and pushing boundaries despite the scrutiny and deeply personal criticism of her appearance and body shape.
- Her determination to return to competitive gymnastics after the challenges of Tokyo – pushing through her fears and mental struggles, confident that she still had more to offer.

*Grace*

- Her courage in speaking openly about her ADHD, offering hope and encouragement to many others facing similar struggles.
- Staying to cheer on her teammates and congratulate her competitors at the Tokyo Olympics despite the intense media scrutiny and her personal mental health struggles.
- Her dignified response to the media criticism following her withdrawal from events at the Tokyo Olympics – using the opportunity to shine a light on the importance of mental health in sports.

*Key Life Lessons:*

- **It's Okay Not to Be Okay Sometimes:** Just as Simone took some time off from gymnastics, it's okay to admit when we need a break. Sometimes, we get caught up in trying to be perfect at everything, whether it's school, sports, or any other

activity. But nobody is perfect, and pushing ourselves too hard can lead to burnout. Taking a step back doesn't mean we're weak; instead, it means we're wise enough to know our limits.
- **Be Willing to Ask for Help:** Feeling sad or just not yourself is completely normal – sharing your feelings with someone you trust can really help. Doing so doesn't make you weak; it makes you human. When Simone struggled in the run-up to the Tokyo Olympics, she didn't feel she could ask for help: *"I thought I could figure it out on my own, but that's sometimes not the case. And that's not something you should feel guilty or ashamed of."*
- **Support Others:** Even when Simone couldn't compete at the Tokyo Olympics, she stayed to cheer on her teammates, showing the importance of being there for your friends. She also uses her global fame to help those less fortunate, reminding us that supporting others is a powerful way to make a difference.
- **Aim for Excellence:** Simone always pushes herself to be the best. She spends countless hours training and perfecting her moves – always challenging herself to leap higher, incorporate more flips and twists, and land more gracefully.
- **Find Balance:** Simone's experience teaches us valuable lessons about balancing excellence with mental well-being. By prioritizing our mental health, taking breaks, practicing self-care, setting realistic goals, asking for help, embracing failure, and celebrating our achievements, we can strive for greatness without sacrificing our well-being.

So, next time you find yourself in a challenging situation, think of Simone. Remember that true strength comes from knowing when to push forward and when to step back. Strive for your dreams and push your limits but remember to take care of yourself along the way. After all, the most important thing is not only how far you go but how you feel along the way.

Next, let's race into the incredible world of a track and field superstar. With her sparkling face paint and lightning-fast legs, her story is not just about winning medals; it's about believing in yourself and never giving up on your dreams, no matter how tough things get.

# 8

# DEEDEE TROTTER

"Every person is capable of being a champion because a champion is simply a person who never gives up."

DeeDee Trotter

In the electrifying world of track and field, DeeDee Trotter's journey stands out —not just for her blazing speed on the track but for her incredible comeback. After a devastating knee injury, almost everyone had written her off, agreeing her career was over, but DeeDee refused to give up. Powered by an unwavering belief in herself, she overcame all obstacles to keep racing towards her dreams.

DeeDee Trotter was born in California on December 8, 1982. In her early years at school, DeeDee wasn't involved in any organized sports. But her energy and competitive spirit shone through, and she would nearly always win the games that she and her school friends played in outdoor recess.

When her parents divorced, DeeDee moved to Georgia, where organized youth sports were very popular. It was here that basketball first captured her heart. She met her best friend on the basketball court; her friend's dad was the coach and taught DeeDee the basics of the game. A natural athlete, DeeDee quickly became a skilled and valued member of the team.

Before long, basketball became DeeDee's true passion. Every year, her team would compete in a tournament at the University of Tennessee (UT), and DeeDee would dream about playing basketball there. At home, DeeDee would watch Pat Summitt, UT's iconic coach, on television – and her desire to join UT and train under Coach Summitt grew stronger. (You may remember Pat Summitt from Tamika Catchings' story — she was Tamika's coach at UT.)

Whenever DeeDee played basketball, coaches were amazed by her speed and suggested she try out for track events. Initially, DeeDee wasn't keen on the idea. Basketball was her first love, and she didn't see herself running track, so she didn't run much in middle school. At high school, with a little push from her coaches and encouragement from a couple of friends who ran summer track, she reluctantly started competing occasionally. Her natural talent was undeniable, and she regularly outperformed other athletes who trained more intensively. DeeDee still didn't really enjoy running, but she had a strong faith; she believed that God had blessed her with this gift, and it was her duty to pursue it. At the State Championships, in her final year at high school, she won the 200-meter indoor and outdoor titles and ran the anchor leg of the 4x400m relay, helping secure a win for her team.

DeeDee's talents on the basketball court and track attracted the attention of many universities. She received letters for both sports from various institutions, including her dream school, UT. She was still assessing her different options when fate intervened.

One evening, after returning from a basketball tournament, DeeDee received an unexpected call from her track coach. He had entered her for a track event just two days later. DeeDee was shocked. Her school basketball team had been performing exceptionally well, and she had been prioritizing basketball practice. Despite having done no recent training for track, her coach persuaded her to participate.

On race day, DeeDee gave it her all, and to everyone's amazement, she won and set a new indoor record. Her stunning performance caught the eye of a UT track coach attending the event, who rushed to speak with DeeDee after the race.

DeeDee explained that she wanted to study at UT, but her dream was to play basketball, not run track. The coach recognized DeeDee's talent and offered her a scholarship, proposing an interesting deal. If DeeDee spent her first year focusing on track, the coach would help her get onto the basketball team. This seemed like a golden opportunity - DeeDee accepted the scholarship on the understanding that she could pursue both sports. However, things didn't turn out as planned.

In her first year at UT, DeeDee's plan fell apart. Her track coach resigned, and the new coaching team refused to honor her agreement with the previous coach. She was told she would lose her scholarship if she attended basketball trials. After exploring other options, DeeDee realized she had little choice but to continue with track. Heartbroken, she realized that her dreams of playing basketball at UT were over.

The next few months were a real struggle for DeeDee. She had to keep training but resented everything about the track program; her heart just wasn't in it. She did what she had to do and nothing more. Then, one day, DeeDee found out she had been entered into a 400m event, a distance she had never raced before – she usually ran shorter races, like the 100m and 200m. She agreed to race but was so angry and frustrated that she jogged around the track. Afterward, one of the coaches came over to talk to her. DeeDee shared how upset she was about not being able to play basketball and how she felt the coaches didn't care about her feelings. The coach explained that while she couldn't get DeeDee into basketball, she wanted to help her enjoy and feel more appreciated in her track events. She came up with a plan: if DeeDee ran the 400m at some events, she could pick her favorite distances at other races. DeeDee agreed.

Not long after, DeeDee was training for a 400m event when some comments from coaches and teammates totally shifted DeeDee's mindset. Trying to be supportive, they told her to do her best and not worry too much about the result. Their words really annoyed DeeDee: she realized they expected her to lose. DeeDee was determined to prove them wrong. Using their doubts as fuel, she flew around the track, winning the race and beating the world leader.

After this victory, DeeDee was given more opportunities to compete in 400m races and nearly always placed in the top 3. She competed in the US trials and came third, winning a place on the US team for the World Championships in Paris. Here, she made it to the semi-finals, and people began talking about her as a rising star.

Back at college, DeeDee still didn't want a career in track. At that time, track and field wasn't seen as glamorous—athletes received little recognition, and the pay wasn't great. However, she began receiving calls asking if she would turn professional. She rejected the first deal, saying the salary was too low. They returned with a better offer: if she could win the 400m at the NCAA, beating the leading athlete, they would propose a much better deal.

DeeDee won the race; she was offered a significantly better deal and became the first female athlete at UT to turn professional before completing four years of college. While at Tennessee, she was the

NCAA 400m runner-up in 2003 and champion in 2004, setting a university record with a time of 50.00 seconds.

From this point on, salaries for women track and field athletes increased significantly.

DeeDee's successes continued at the 2004 Olympic Games in Athens, coming fifth in the 400m Olympic final and being part of the USA gold medal-winning 4 x 400m team. Over the next few years, DeeDee continued to race internationally, winning medals in 400m and 4 x 400m events.

Fast forward to 2008: DeeDee was at the top of her game, training hard for the upcoming Olympics in Beijing. She was in excellent shape, and everyone believed she had a real shot at winning gold. However, one day, out of the blue, DeeDee felt a sharp pain in her knee. Scans revealed a serious knee injury. Doctors explained she would need surgery and warned that it was a new procedure with low success rates; it was unlikely DeeDee would recover to compete at an elite level again. This was devastating news, but DeeDee wasn't ready to give up. Knowing the surgery could end her career, she decided to delay it until after the Games.

Determined to make the Olympic team, she worked intensively with doctors and therapists to strengthen her knee. The next few months were incredibly tough for DeeDee. She came last in her next few races but refused to quit. Eventually, she was told she couldn't compete in elite races anymore; she just wasn't good enough. Still, DeeDee refused to give up: a voice inside her kept saying, *"I can, I must, I will keep going."* Even though people were writing her off, the belief in her heart to keep going was stronger. She continued training and raced at smaller events.

When the Olympic trials came around, DeeDee had a string of losses behind her. She needed to finish in the top three to earn a place on the team. Against all odds, DeeDee made it through the first three races, qualifying for the trial finals and surprising everyone. She was in serious pain but refused to let it show. In the final race, she found herself in 7th place at the 300-meter mark and almost gave up. But something inside her told her to keep going, to keep believing in herself. And that's what she did. She picked up the pace and clinched third place, securing her ticket to the Beijing Olympics.

Unfortunately, DeeDee's knee injury flared up at the Olympics, and she didn't qualify for the 400m final. She had been chosen for the 4 x 400m relay team but realized her injury could jeopardize her team's chance of winning gold. DeeDee put the team first - she pulled out of the race, and one of her teammates took her place. The USA went on to win gold. DeeDee returned from the Olympics without a medal but knowing that her sacrifice had helped her team achieve greatness.

After the 2008 Olympics, DeeDee returned home and had her knee surgery. The next few years were some of the toughest years of her career as she worked to return to racing at an elite level. Despite her determination, she found herself losing race after race, and it seemed like everyone—from fans to sponsors—thought her days as a champion were over. But DeeDee didn't let this break her spirit. Instead, she listened to a little voice inside her that she named her "inner champion," which reminded her to keep going no matter what. She viewed each loss as an opportunity to learn. DeeDee was determined to prove the doubters wrong and return stronger than ever for the 2012 Olympics.

As she grew physically stronger, DeeDee also worked hard to build her mental toughness. She used positive affirmations to drown out any doubts and overcome the mental blocks holding her back. DeeDee also adopted a new ritual: wearing face paint when competing. She called this her "war paint," saying it made her feel like a strong warrior ready to conquer any challenge that came her way.

DeeDee secured her spot at the 2012 London Olympics with a stunning second-place finish in the US trials. At the Games, wearing her signature war paint, she powered her way to a bronze medal in the individual 400m event and helped the US women's team win gold in the 4 x 400m relay. DeeDee ran an incredible first leg, building a lead of nearly ten meters before passing the baton, setting her team up for victory. Her remarkable comeback captured the hearts of fans and drew significant media attention, earning her the nickname 'Glitter Face Warrior.'

For DeeDee, winning the bronze medal in the 400m in London is her gold medal moment. She knew how hard she had worked, how many challenges she had overcome, how many times she had had to pick herself up and keep going. She often says her bronze medal is just *a 'different shade of gold.'*

DeeDee was valued and respected by her teammates for her dedication and team spirit. She often speaks of three key aspects of teamwork: appreciating and respecting the roles of other team members, constantly improving your skills to be an asset to the team and focusing not on individual glory but on the team's collective success.

DeeDee Trotter hung up her running spikes in 2016, but she hasn't slowed down a bit! Like the other amazing women in this book, DeeDee stays active and involved. She passionately speaks out against the use of performance-enhancing drugs in sports and engages in various charitable efforts, including distributing shoes and providing meals to people experiencing homelessness in Florida. She founded "Running for the People," a non-profit that organizes running events to support, encourage, and inspire those in need. DeeDee is also a powerful motivational speaker who uses her life story to inspire others to overcome their challenges. Additionally, she has fulfilled her childhood dream of becoming a professional pastry chef! Now, she's the head pastry chef at a prestigious golf club and operates a thriving bakery.

DeeDee's journey from a reluctant track athlete to an Olympic medalist is more than just a tale of athletic achievement; it teaches perseverance, faith, and resilience. She shows us that a champion is not defined by victories alone but by the courage to continue despite failures and setbacks.

*Instances of Grit and Grace:*

*Grit*

- DeeDee's determination to make the US team for the Beijing Olympics despite her serious knee injury. Racing in smaller events when she was excluded from elite races and persevering through rounds of qualifying races at the Olympic trials despite serious pain from her knee.
- Her remarkable comeback at the 2012 London Olympics, astonishing everyone when she won the bronze medal.

*Grace*

- Putting the team first at the Beijing Olympics by giving up her place on the 4x400m relay team, recognizing that her teammate was in a stronger position to ensure a gold medal for the team.
- Supporting and encouraging other athletes at race meets, choosing mutual respect over rivalry.

*Key Life Lessons:*

- **Never Stop Believing in Yourself:** DeeDee's story shows us that even when things get super tough, believing in yourself is key. After getting hurt, facing many defeats, and people believing her career was over, DeeDee refused to give up. She kept believing she would race at an elite level again.
- **Define Your Version of Success:** DeeDee's journey teaches us that success isn't just about crossing the finish line first. What truly matters is the progress you have made and the obstacles you have overcome.
- **Be Willing to Try:** When DeeDee injured her knee, she wasn't sure if she could make the Olympic team, but knew she had to try. She realized that not trying would mean failing for

sure. You never know what amazing things you could achieve until you try.
- **Put the Team First:** DeeDee Trotter made a big decision during the Olympics when she gave up her place in the relay team. Being a true team player sometimes means putting the group's success above your own. DeeDee teaches us that real strength lies in making choices that benefit everyone, not just ourselves.
- **Affirmations Can Help Overcome Mental Blocks:** DeeDee used affirmations to help her push past negative thoughts as she worked to return to elite competition.

So, next time you face challenges or setbacks, think of DeeDee. Remember her determination to keep trying, her refusal to give up even when the odds seemed stacked against her. Let her story inspire you to push through your struggles, keeping faith in yourself every step of the way.

Let's now dive into the story of an incredible athlete whose waves of determination and strength have redefined what it means to be a swimming champion.

## 9

# KATIE LEDECKY

"Chase your own dreams, not the dreams of others."

Katie Ledecky

Katie Ledecky's story is a remarkable tale of dedication, endurance, and shattering expectations. Her tale isn't just about gliding through water or stacking up gold medals—it's about determination, discipline, and the refusal to settle for anything less than greatness. With more medals than any other female swimmer, Katie is a true inspiration who knows how to set a goal and stay laser-focused to achieve it.

Katie was born on March 17, 1997, in Maryland, just outside Washington D.C. She started swimming when she was very young. Her mother had been a competitive swimmer at college and wanted her children to enjoy swimming as much as she did. When Katie was six, she and her older brother, Michael, joined a swim club to meet new friends. One of Katie's first recorded moments in the pool is a cute home video showing her clinging to the lane lines during a race.

Katie's love for swimming was undeniable. She would wake up early to watch her brother train before her turn. Each evening, she would write her swimming goals on sticky notes and stick them around her room, dreaming of the day she would achieve them. An ear infection almost kept her from reaching one of her first goals—swimming across the pool without stopping.

*"I've always set goals. When I was a kid, I would write them down, and I would work toward them, and that's still pretty much what I do."*

The next year, Katie took her goal setting to the next level. She began jotting down "Want Times," her target times for races in the eight-and-under category, on a piece of paper and kept it on her bedside table. After each race, she would record her actual times, calculate the difference from her goals, and update her list.

Katie dedicated as much time as possible to swimming, training hard to improve her technique and fitness. Katie learned early on that setbacks are not failures but stepping stones to greater achievements. This mindset was crucial during her early competitions, where she experienced defeats and victories. Each race taught her something new about herself and her swimming technique, driving her to keep improving.

Competitive swimming training is incredibly demanding and takes a lot of dedication. Imagine waking up while it's still dark outside to train before school, diving into a cold pool when most people are still sleeping. Swimmers like Katie spend hours every day in the pool, practicing their strokes, perfecting their turns, and building their endurance. Training requires not only physical strength but also mental toughness to keep going, especially on days when you're tired, or things aren't going your way. Katie's family supported and encouraged her; they were always there on the sidelines, cheering her on and helping her through the tough times.

Katie's passion and discipline caught the eye of her coach, Yuri Suguiyama, who encouraged her to adopt a more aggressive kicking style, a technique often used by elite male swimmers but less common among females. Before starting high school, her hard work paid off dramatically at the US Junior Championships, where she won the 400-, 800- and 1,500-meter freestyle events, marking her as a rising star in the swimming world.

A year later, Katie qualified for the 2012 Olympic trials. She astonished everyone by winning the 800-meter freestyle, earning her place on the US team for the 2012 Olympic Games in London. In the build-up to the Olympics, she remembers visualizing the race and winning gold before she went to bed each night; slowly, she started to believe it was possible.

In London, Katie Ledecky stunned the swimming world by winning the gold medal and setting a new American record in the 800-meter freestyle. Her incredible performance showed everyone that age is just a number, and if you put your mind to something and work hard, you can achieve greatness. This win showed not only Katie's physical strength but also her remarkable mental toughness. It was a dream come true and the beginning of her journey to becoming one of the most celebrated swimmers in the world.

After her triumph in London, Katie's new coach identified several areas for improvement, recognizing Katie could reach even greater heights. Katie trained harder than ever, pushing her limits and constantly striving to improve and excel. Every year, she and her coach set challenging goals that often felt daunting. Initially, Katie struggled to see how she would achieve them, but she always surpassed them with hard work and determination. She always kept her goals top of mind, even writing her target times on her swim float for a while.

She focused not on beating other swimmers but on improving her own times, putting a lot of pressure on herself:

*"I approach each race with the belief in myself that I can swim a best time, and that's pretty darn tough."*

Katie frequently trained with male swimmers, who were generally stronger, to motivate and challenge her further. When a race didn't turn out as expected, she would review her performance, learn from her mistakes, and dedicate training time to ensure better results next time.

What makes Katie even more amazing is her determination to continue her education despite her punishing training routine. While winning medals and setting records, she also excelled in school, proving that you can simultaneously shine in sports and academics. Katie attended Stanford University, one of the top schools in the US, where she balanced a demanding swimming schedule with her psychology coursework. She had to be highly organized, rising early for swim practice and then dedicating time to study. She loved being part of the university swim team and attending classes with friends; it helped keep her grounded and sometimes feel like a typical teenager. Katie's dedication to swimming and school demonstrates that with hard work and good planning, you can achieve great things in both areas. Although her busy swimming schedule did mean she missed certain events, including her graduation ceremony, which she celebrated poolside, wearing her cap and gown!

Katie is a swimming superstar. Her gold medal in London was just the start of her Olympic success. Katie has won fourteen Olympic medals – nine golds, four silvers, and one bronze. At the 2024 Paris Games, Katie achieved an extraordinary feat by winning the 800m freestyle for the fourth time in a row. After her triumphs in Paris, she became the most decorated female US Olympic athlete. At World Championships, she has claimed an impressive 21 gold medals. Katie has repeatedly broken world records. Her remarkable power, unwavering endurance, and positive attitude have made her one of the greatest swimmers ever.

Katie's story shows us that while natural talent plays a role, a strong mindset and work ethic are crucial to achieving your goals. Doing what you love is just as important - Katie often shares how much she enjoys swimming, whether it's the rigorous training, racing, or cheering for her teammates.

Katie Ledecky is not just a champion in the pool but also a true team player and a great sport. Despite all her victories, she remains down-to-earth, always quick to credit her coaches, family, and teammates for their part in her success. During the Tokyo Olympics, when Ariarne Titmus took gold in a race Katie had hoped to win, Katie was the first to congratulate her. She deeply cares about her teammates, always cheering them on and celebrating their achievements. Katie's actions remind us that being supportive and kind is just as important as winning.

Away from the pool and university, Katie uses her fame to support different charities and projects. She's super passionate about inspiring girls to learn more about STEM subjects - science, technology, engineering, and math (STEM) - and believes getting more girls involved in these areas is important. She also supports several Catholic charities close to her home. Given her love of swimming, it's not surprising she helps other swimmers as well – she supported the Refugee Olympic team at the Tokyo Olympics and is a volunteer coach for athletes at the University of Florida.

***Instances of Grit & Grace:***

***Grit***

- Katie's early mornings and rigorous training - honing her

strokes, perfecting her turns, and building her fitness – all before the school day began.
- Setting very challenging goals and working tirelessly to achieve them.

## *Grace*

- Katie shines as a supportive teammate who frequently supports her teammates and celebrates their victories as if they were her own. She cherishes her close relationships with her team, often highlighting how their support contributes to her achievements.
- Congratulating her rivals on their achievements, despite her feelings of disappointment.
- Always making time for her young fans. Katie is kind, approachable, and happy to inspire and encourage the next generation of girls in swimming and other fields.

## *Key Life Lessons:*

- **The Power of Visualization:** Before each race, Katie Ledecky uses visualization to mentally prepare. She imagines each stroke, turn, and finish, picturing exactly how she wants to swim. This technique helps her stay calm and focused when the real race begins, allowing her to perform at her best.
- **Set Goals and Stay Focused**: Katie's journey teaches us the power of having clear goals. From writing her 'Want Times' on a piece of paper as a young girl to aiming for Olympic gold, Katie always kept her goals in mind and worked hard to reach them, no matter what. If you set clear goals and don't give up, you can do amazing things!
- **Cheer Others On:** Success is best when shared. Despite her incredible success, Katie was always there to cheer on her teammates and celebrate their successes.
- **Have fun**: Achieving your biggest dreams is much easier if you're having fun, so do something you enjoy! Katie talks

about how much fun she's always had swimming, even when the training was hard. In an interview for Adidas, she says: *"I would just encourage young kids to find something that they really love, that they enjoy, whether that's sport or something else, and try to be the best that you can be at it and enjoy it."*

Maybe you're not aiming for an Olympic medal (or perhaps you are!), but whatever your dreams, keep Katie's story in mind and remember her words:

*"Don't sell yourself short. You are more capable than you think."*

We're back on the soccer pitch next to meet an incredible athlete who broke barriers and inspired millions – becoming a role model for girls everywhere.

# 10

# MIA HAMM

"Failure happens all the time. It happens every day in practice. What makes you better is how you react to it."

Mia Hamm

This story is about another soccer superstar, Mia Hamm, a brilliant player and two-time Olympic gold medalist. Mia battled feelings of fear, worry, and shyness to conquer the pitch with confidence. From wanting to blend into the background to shining as bright as a soccer pitch's lights, Mia Hamm has paved the path for future generations of female athletes. Let's kick things off and explore how Mia Hamm became a global soccer sensation.

Mia Hamm was born in the United States on March 17, 1972. Growing up in a big family, she faced a challenge early on—she was born with a partial club foot and had to wear corrective shoes as a toddler. Mia's father was an Air Force pilot, and her mother was a dancer. Mia's full name was Mariel Margaret, but she was nicknamed Mia by her mother, after the ballet dancer Mia Slavenska. Mia's mother hoped her daughter would be a dancer too, but Mia refused, walking out after her second ballet lesson!

Mia's dad's job required the family to move frequently. When Mia was about one year old, the family moved to Florence, Italy. It was here that their love for soccer truly blossomed. A neighbor often took Mia's dad to soccer games, and soon, the entire family caught the soccer bug. In Italy, where soccer is like a religion, it was hard not to get swept up in the excitement.

The Hamm family returned to the US when Mia was four years old. Not long after, they adopted two boys—Martin, a newborn, and Garrett, who was eight years old. Garrett was very sporty, and Mia idolized him. He became not just a brother but also a role model.

Mia's father helped at the local soccer club, refereeing matches and coaching Garrett and Mia's older sister. Mia would watch from the sidelines, counting down the days until she turned five and could officially join the fun.

Growing up, Garrett was incredibly supportive of Mia. He practiced with her and persuaded his friends to let her play with them. She credits him with encouraging her in sports. When she was little, Mia was so fast and athletic that Garrett used her as a "secret weapon" when they played games like Capture the Flag. His belief in her abilities gave Mia the confidence to chase her dreams. In seventh grade, Mia joined a boys' soccer team, and her impressive skills soon led to her being accepted by the boys.

However, Mia, now one of the greatest soccer players in history, had her own struggles growing up. She wasn't always the confident athlete we see on TV. In fact, Mia was very shy as a child. She found it hard to make friends and often walked through the school halls with her head down, fidgeting and worrying about how she looked. Her voice was so soft that sometimes you could hardly hear her.

Soccer became her refuge, her safe place where she didn't have to feel nervous or shy. No matter where she went, Mia felt like she belonged if there was a soccer ball. Through soccer, she found a way to express herself - running, kicking, and giving her all on the field allowed her to shake off those nervous feelings and be herself.

Over the next few years, Mia worked tirelessly to hone her skills as a striker. She understood that raw talent alone wasn't enough. What truly set her apart was her relentless drive to get better every single day. She constantly trained, practiced new techniques, and fine-tuned every aspect of her game.

At times, Mia felt lonely and out of place. As the boys grew older, they became less enthusiastic about having a girl on their team, and playing with the local girls didn't feel right either. She couldn't understand why some girls wore makeup to play soccer or got distracted by boys during the game!

Things started looking up for Mia when she tried out for an Olympic development girls' team at 14. She was accepted, and six months later, Mia was promoted to the women's team. At just 15 years old, Mia Hamm became the youngest US women's national soccer team player. She was suddenly among like-minded women, talented players who trained hard and played even harder. Mia was overjoyed and more excited than ever to pursue the sport she loved.

After high school, Mia enrolled at the University of North Carolina and soon became an integral part of the university's soccer team, helping the Tar Heels win four NCAA Women's Championships in five years. During her time with the Tar Heels, she scored an incredible 103 goals, and the team only lost one game of the 95 she played. She was recognized as an All-American athlete and named the Atlantic Coast Conference (ACC) Player of the Year three times. Mia's presence on the team, with her incredible soccer skills, inspiring leadership and relentless drive, motivated and uplifted everyone around her. While at North Carolina, she evolved into one of the brightest stars in women's soccer.

Mia took time out from college soccer in 1991 to play in the first-ever FIFA Women's World Cup in China. She was the youngest player on the team and scored the game-winning goal in their opening match. The US went on to win the tournament, defeating Norway 1-0 in the final.

When the Women's United Soccer Association (WUSA) launched in 2001 as the first professional women's soccer league in the US, Mia was a founding member. She played for the Washington Freedom from 2001- 2003, and was one of the league's biggest stars, frequently appearing in its ads and promotions.

Despite her success on the soccer field, Mia often struggled with nerves before games. She realized these feelings could affect her performance, so she developed a strategy to manage them. During warm-ups, she would channel all her thoughts and energy into one specific aspect of her game, such as planning her first touch or focusing on her acceleration. This approach helped her calm her nerves and gave her something to focus on in the minutes before the match started.

Mia is widely recognized in the soccer community for her exceptional work ethic and unwavering determination. Early one morning, her coach, Anson Dorrance, was on his way to work when he spotted Mia working out, covered in sweat. Inspired, he went into his office and wrote a note that coaches around the globe still quote, years later: *"The vision of a champion is someone who is bent over, drenched in sweat, at the point of exhaustion, when nobody else is watching."*

Mia's world was turned upside down when her adored older brother, Garrett, was diagnosed with a rare blood disease at the age of 16. Initially managed with medication, the condition forced him to give up contact sports, a crushing blow for such a talented athlete. Eventually, Garrett needed a bone marrow transplant. To help cover the costs of her brother's operation, Mia organized a special benefit game. Nearly all her US women's national teammates played to support her. The money raised was shared between a children's hospital and her brother's medical expenses.

Although the operation was successful, Garrett suffered complications and tragically passed away at the age of 28. Playing soccer and the support of her teammates helped Mia through this heartbreaking time. Two years later, Mia established the Mia Hamm Foundation to raise funds and awareness for bone marrow transplants and to support patients and their families.

Mia played with the US Women's National Soccer Team for 17 years, scoring 158 goals, making 144 assists, and building one of the biggest fan bases of any American athlete. She helped the team win the Women's World Cup in 1991 and 1999 and Olympic gold medals in 1996 and 2004. Mia was named FIFA's "World Player of the Year" in 2001 and 2002, and in 2013, she became the first woman inducted into the World Football Hall of Fame. With her lightning-quick feet and ice-cool finishes, Mia broke barriers while inspiring a new generation of fans and players.

Throughout her career, Mia consistently stressed the importance of her teammates. They were the driving force that pushed her to constantly improve. *"I wanted to be the best player I could be so the team could be the best team it could be."*

As Mia's success grew, the impact of her achievements began to ripple outwards. Her talent and hard work helped bring women's soccer into the spotlight, inspiring countless young girls to take up soccer. Mia's influence soon reached far beyond the soccer fields, showing that women could excel in areas often dominated by men. Her achievements challenged old-fashioned ideas and helped create more acceptance and support for women playing sports.

Her status as a sporting legend and role model for women reached new heights when she appeared in a famous commercial alongside basketball icon Michael Jordan. In "Anything You Can Do, I Can Do Better," the two superstars competed in various sports, sending a groundbreaking message that women could compete with men.

Mia blazed a trail for future generations of girls, showing them what's possible and encouraging them to believe that female athletes belong in the spotlight.

Following her retirement from professional soccer in 2004, Mia has dedicated her time and energy to the Mia Hamm Foundation. The foundation now has a dual mission: raising funds and awareness for bone marrow transplants, as well as increasing opportunities for young women in sports.

Mia also gives motivational speeches, championing gender equality and sharing her story along with insights on leadership and teamwork. Considering she once struggled with shyness and spoke so softly that she was hard to hear, her journey is truly amazing.

***Instances of Grit and Grace:***

***Grit***

- Her work ethic, which inspired the note from her coach: *"The vision of a champion is someone who is bent over, drenched in sweat, at the point of exhaustion, when nobody else is watching."*
- Staying true to her soccer dreams, despite feeling lonely and out of place growing up.
- Refusing to let her shyness stand in the way of achieving her goals or stop her from becoming a vocal advocate for women's soccer.

*Grace*

- Celebrating team success over personal glory – Mia was known for her humility and team-first attitude. When accepting awards, she focused her speeches on thanking her teammates and coaches, attributing her success to their support rather than claiming the spotlight for herself.
- Organizing a benefit game to raise funds for her brother's medical expenses and a local children's hospital.
- Giving back to the community, Mia now uses her fame to inspire and mentor young female athletes, promote women's football, and raise funds and awareness for bone marrow transplants.

*Key Life Lessons:*

- **Be Willing to Step Out of Your Comfort Zone**: Mia's story shows that doing things you find challenging can lead to growth and success.
- **It's Okay to Be Nervous**: Just like Mia, everyone feels nervous at times, especially before important events. Mia calmed her nerves by focusing on one aspect of her game. There are plenty of ways to help calm nerves and manage anxiety: it may take trying a few before finding one that works best for you.
- **Embrace the Importance of Teamwork:** Mia believes that the strength of a team lies in understanding that everyone is equally important. Achieving a shared goal requires every member's contribution. Mia always credited her teammates for driving her to improve. She believed that working together made everyone stronger and always strived to be her best for the team's benefit. Even individual stars need the support and collaboration of others to shine brightly.

The next time you kick a soccer ball or face a tough challenge, think of Mia. Let her journey inspire you to push forward and stay committed to your dreams. Knowing that it's possible to overcome difficulties and shine can make all the difference.

For our next story, we're staying in the US but moving to the racetrack to meet an incredible woman determined to succeed in a male-dominated sport.

# 11

# DANICA PATRICK

"You need to do what you truly enjoy and then you'll be willing to go the extra mile to be successful at it"

Danica Patrick

Danica Patrick's journey is filled with many twists and turns, a tale of determination, resilience, and breaking barriers. Her story is not just about going fast or winning races—it's a narrative of breaking speed limits and stereotypes, a true inspiration for anyone who dares to dream big and drive hard toward their goals. It's like a giant green light telling us all to go for our dreams, even if they seem far away.

Have you ever been told you can't do something, or you don't fit in because of who you are? That's exactly where Danica started in the world of racing, which is very much a boys' club. She faced doubts, side-eyes, and people waiting for her to slip up, all because she dared to join their race. In a sport dominated by men, Danica had to fight not only to win races but also to earn respect and recognition for her driving skills.

Danica was born on March 25, 1982, and grew up in a small town in Illinois. Cars and racing were part of her life from early on. Her father loved racing, and Danica would often watch her dad compete in tournaments, racing around the track, and long to do the same. By age 10, she and her sister Brooke were zipping around in go-karts – hands tight on the steering wheel, eyes sparkling with excitement and the pure joy of speed.

Danica and Brooke started competing soon after. Despite crashing into a wall during her first race, Danica was unfazed and eager to start racing again as soon as her go-kart was repaired. Brooke also competed for a few months but decided to give up after crashing a few times. With the support and encouragement of her family, Danica kept going. Danica's father spent time teaching her all he knew about cars and racing. He kept challenging her by entering her into more competitive races as she progressed. Slowly, her skills and confidence grew.

After winning multiple regional and national go-kart titles, Danica was offered the opportunity to race in England. With her parents' encouragement, she left school at 16 and moved to England. Although it sounds exciting, it was a tough and lonely time for her. As the only girl on her new team, Danica faced constant criticism and was often ignored by the boys and coaches. She recalls a practice session where she was quicker than the boys. Instead of receiving praise, the coach criticized the boys for letting a girl beat them. Despite the lack of support, Danica stayed in England for three years, honing her racing skills and mental resilience. Her persistence paid off: In 2000, she secured second place in the Formula Ford Festival, the best result for a woman or an American.

In 2001, Danica returned home to America and started looking for a job in racing and sponsorship. During her time in England, Danica had become friends with Bobby Rahal, a former racing driver who had started a racing team when he retired and had met up with him a few times once back in the US. Danica remembers being told that if Bobby confirmed she'd be on his team, it would help her land her first full-time sponsor. Unsure about asking such a bold question, Danica hesitated. However, the person she was speaking with encouraged her to ask directly. At their next meeting in Milwaukee, Danica gathered her courage, took a deep breath, approached Bobby, and asked if he would sign a letter of intent stating she'd drive Atlantic for him, which would help her secure a sponsor. He paused, looked around, and then agreed. Her direct approach had paid off!

In 2002, Danica Patrick signed a deal to race for Bobby Rahal's team - Rahal Letterman Lanigan Racing. After competing in a few races in the Barber Dodge Pro Series, she moved up to the Toyota Atlantic Championship in 2003. Danica had a solid run in the series: She earned one pole position and regularly finished in the top three but didn't win a race. In 2004, she finished third overall in the Championship.

In 2005, Danica Patrick secured her spot in the highly competitive Indianapolis 500, one of the most prestigious car races in the US. At that time, only three other women had ever qualified for this event. This was a big moment for Danica; she had watched IndyCar regularly while growing up and often dreamed of competing. During practice, she impressed everyone by clocking the fastest time. On race day, she made history as the first woman to lead the race three times; she led for 19 laps, ultimately finishing fourth.

In 2008, Danica became the first woman to win an IndyCar race, taking the Indy Japan 300 when the leading competitors were forced to stop for fuel in the race's closing laps.

In 2010, Danica switched to NASCAR, driving stock cars. She loved this style of racing, which reminded her of her time racing go-karts. However, as Danica's fame and success grew, she found herself under intense media scrutiny. Much of it was critical – questioning her right to compete as a woman in a male-dominated sport or focusing on her appearance rather than her racing achievements. Danica felt incredibly frustrated by this – she wanted people to believe in her and her racing abilities.

Over time, Danica realized that we can't control what others think or say about us. What we can control is our behavior and the choices we make. This insight shifted her focus from trying to change other people's opinions to building a circle of supportive friends who had her back. By trusting in her own abilities and shutting out the negativity, Danica became one of the most successful women in the history of car racing.

Training and competing at the highest levels required sacrifices, long hours, and mental toughness. Her career was punctuated with exhilarating highs and challenging lows—crashes, mechanical failures, and races where nothing went right. Yet, Danica saw each setback as a learning opportunity, a chance to refine her skills and come back stronger.

Here are a few of her many incredible achievements: She was recently named one of the most influential people in sports. She made history as the first woman to win an IndyCar race, breaking several records. She raced IndyCars for seven seasons and was voted the most popular driver for six of those seasons. Additionally, she broke barriers as the first woman to start the Daytona 500 and to host the ESPY Awards ceremony, which honors outstanding athletic performances.

Off the track, Danica uses her celebrity status to advocate for causes close to her heart. She champions women in sports, helping to pave the way for the next generation of female athletes. Danica is also involved in various projects that empower young women and promote physical fitness and healthy living. Additionally, she supports initiatives for breast cancer awareness and helps children and war veterans, using her platform to highlight these vital issues.

Danica's journey teaches us the power of never giving up, being yourself, and having the courage to break through barriers and change what people think is possible. It reminds us that we can achieve incredible things when we don't follow society's rules and instead choose to follow our dreams.

*Instances of Grit & Grace:*

*Grit*

- Moving to England when she was 16 - being the only girl on the team, often ignored and criticized by teammates. This was a tough and lonely time for Danica, but she refused to give up and stayed in the UK, rather than returning to her family in the US.
- Her steadfast determination to keep going, despite the negativity and criticism she faced competing in such a male-dominated sport.

*Grace*

- Remaining professional and poised during media interviews – even when interviewers questioned her capabilities and place in a predominantly male sport.
- Her work empowering girls to believe in themselves and advocating for more gender equality for women in sport.

*Key Life Lessons:*

- **Dare to be Different**: Sometimes, Danica was the only woman competing at an event. She was fearless and brave and never gave up on her dreams. As Danica says: *"have your own path, that's what makes you unique, that's what makes you interesting."*

- **Don't be Afraid to Ask for What You Want:** Sometimes, you need to be brave and ask tough or awkward questions—just like Danica did when she directly asked Bobby Rahal about joining his racing team.
- **Focus on What You Can Control**: When faced with criticism or unkind words, remember how Danica learned to handle negativity: we can't control what other people say and do, but we can control our thoughts and actions.
- **Be Willing to Take Risks**: In Danica's words, *"Take those chances, and you can achieve greatness, whereas if you go conservative, you'll never know."*

Whether your dream is speeding around a racetrack, exploring the mysteries of outer space, or discovering new things in a lab, let Danica's journey inspire you to believe that nothing is out of reach. It's all about pursuing your goals, believing in yourself, and daring to be different.

In the next chapter, we travel to the UK to explore the incredible journey of a Paralympic powerhouse whose achievements have redefined the possibilities for athletes with disabilities. Let's go…

# 12

# DAME SARAH STOREY

"If you feel upset when you fail, then let that build your determination and, most importantly, don't be down-hearted, just think of failing as an opportunity to learn where to improve."

Dame Sarah Storey

It's now time to meet Dame Sarah Storey, a girl with only one hand who turned her challenges into incredible success. From dreaming of the Olympics at six years old to becoming an Olympic champion in not one but two sports—swimming and cycling—Sarah's journey from a young girl with a disability to a world-renowned athlete demonstrates that with determination, bravery, and an unstoppable spirit, anything is possible. Get ready to be inspired by a true hero who shows us that no matter what life throws our way, we have the power to conquer it and achieve our dreams.

Born in England on October 26, 1977, with only one functioning hand, Sarah grew up in a family that never made her feel like her disability was a big deal. Her grandmother, who worked in disability services, supported individuals with far greater challenges. She frequently reassured Sarah that her disability didn't have to define her and that others would barely notice it if she didn't draw attention to it.

This perspective was a cornerstone of Sarah's upbringing. Growing up, she had a few gadgets to help her do simple things, like eating with a knife and fork, but she was never treated differently in the family. Her parents were active scout leaders, and the family led an outdoorsy lifestyle filled with camping trips and adventurous activities.

From a young age, Sarah was very sporty and refused to let her missing hand hold her back. She loved playing catch in the backyard and quickly became an expert at catching with one hand, earning her a spot on the regional netball team. Sarah avidly watched the Olympics and tried various sports to see where her talents shone the brightest, hoping she would make it to the Olympics one day. By the age of eight, Sarah was the fastest swimmer in her school, beating pupils three years older.

When Sarah was 10, she joined a local swimming club to train more seriously. A coach told her she was too old to start swimming competitively and that her missing hand would hold her back. Determined to prove them wrong, Sarah trained intensively, getting up at 5 a.m. to swim before school and returning for more training afterward. Within two years, she was outperforming everyone in her age group. Despite her successes, frustration built inside Sarah. No matter how hard she tried, she could never quite make the qualifying times for the National Junior Championships.

One day, everything changed. While flicking through a newspaper, Sarah stumbled upon an article about a young woman with one arm preparing for the Paralympics. Sarah's eyes lit up with curiosity and excitement. Could this be a path for her too? Intrigued, she approached her coach to ask more about these Games. Her coach explained the purpose behind the Paralympics and encouraged her to write to the organizers to see if she might qualify.

Sarah took the advice to heart and wrote a letter to the woman in charge, detailing her situation and expressing her interest. Weeks turned into months without any reply. It would have been easy for Sarah to feel disheartened, to think that she wasn't good enough or didn't meet the criteria. But instead of giving up, Sarah chose persistence. Sarah kept sending letters, each time including her improved swim times.

Eighteen months later, Sarah received a reply. The letter said that Sarah looked like a fast swimmer and invited her to attend a regional competition three weeks later. This was her chance.

Sarah stunned the coaches at the gala, winning all her races and earning an invitation to a training weekend for the British Paralympic swim team. Here, the pool was divided into six lanes. The fastest swimmers were placed in lane 1 and the slowest in lane 6. Sarah found herself in lane 6 initially. By the end of the morning session, she had moved up the lanes and was leading lane 1, the fastest lane. Her strong desire to push herself and see how fast she could swim amazed the coaches. At just 14, she was picked to represent Great Britain at the Paralympics in Barcelona. Her dream was coming true.

For many, participating in such a prestigious event at a young age might feel daunting. However, Sarah refused to be intimidated by the grandeur of the Games. Instead, she approached it as just another swimming gala, choosing to focus on the fun aspect—curious and excited to see how fast she could swim against some of the best athletes in the world.

Her strategy worked wonders. At the Barcelona Paralympic Games, Sarah won six medals: two golds, three silvers, and one bronze. Her performance left both spectators and fellow athletes in awe. She loved every moment of the experience and left with a clear sense of purpose: She knew this was what she wanted to do for the rest of her life.

Returning to school after the Paralympics was a difficult time for Sarah. While her school was proud of her success, they didn't want Sarah to get distracted by her achievements, as she had important exams approaching. Teachers allowed her to bring her medals in for one day but asked her to leave them at home after that and not talk about her achievements too much. They believed this would be the best way to balance her studies and blossoming athletic career.

However, balancing everything wasn't easy. Sarah juggled rigorous training sessions with schoolwork, leaving little time for typical teenage activities like sleepovers or hanging out with friends. Every morning at 5:30 a.m. she'd hit the pool, training until 8:00 a.m. Coaches were strict about completing the full session, and Sarah was no exception. After training, she'd rush to get dressed and often arrived at school with damp hair, a small but telling sign of her dedication.

Other girls didn't understand her commitment or why she couldn't hang out with them much; they assumed she thought she was better than them because of her swimming success. They began to bully her, making fun of her wet hair and talking about her behind her back. The gossip and exclusion escalated, with classmates moving chairs around in classrooms to leave her out.

This was a difficult and lonely time for Sarah, and she turned to her parents for support. They encouraged her to stay strong, reminding her that school would only last a few more years, whereas her athletic career could go on for much longer. They helped her see that, while she couldn't change other people's opinions, she always had control over her actions and reactions. They encouraged her to focus on her schoolwork and training and think of her supportive friends at the swimming club. This perspective helped Sarah see beyond the immediate challenges.

*"It was a lonely existence at school, but because I had this other life where my swimming friends were, where my swimming career was, and the aspirations I had, it was worth it to suck it up. I knew that my career in sport would last a lot longer than bullying at school."*

The bullying took a toll on Sarah; she developed an eating disorder and lost a significant amount of weight. Her mother took her to a doctor who explained the importance of good nutrition for peak performance. The doctor warned Sarah that not eating properly could affect her chances of competing for her country. These words had a profound impact on Sarah, helping her understand that she needed to nourish her body and take care of herself if she wanted to keep competing at an elite level.

Sarah decided it was time to take charge of her well-being. She kept a food diary, which she reviewed with her doctor and coaches. Together, they designed a meal plan to help Sarah perform at her best. This new approach enabled Sarah to manage her eating habits healthily. Since then, Sarah has used her experience to help other athletes struggling with eating disorders, helping them change how they think about food.

Despite her struggles at school, Sarah's sporting successes continued. At the World Para Swimming Championships in 1994, she won two gold medals, two silver medals, and one bronze medal, followed by three golds, one silver, and one bronze at the 1996 Atlanta Paralympic Games. These were incredible achievements, given the challenges she had faced.

However, more obstacles were just around the corner. After finishing school, Sarah was looking forward to university. She spent a lot of time researching universities to work out which would best allow her to balance her academic studies and elite swimming training. It was no small task, but she wanted to ensure she had the best of both worlds.

However, when Sarah started at university, things didn't go as expected. The head swimming coach refused to train her, saying he only worked with Olympic swimmers, not Paralympic athletes like Sarah. Shocked and frustrated, Sarah refused to give up, determined to find a solution. She booked times to use a lane in the pool and trained herself for two years. Balancing academics and self-coaching was tough; eventually, the pressure became too much. She decided to move back home to join her old swimming club and commute to university, a choice that meant lots of traveling alongside her swimming training and studies.

It was exhausting, and Sarah hit another setback. She contracted post-viral fatigue syndrome, leaving her constantly exhausted. Doctors warned her that without rest, she might permanently damage her heart and never compete again. For six weeks, all she could do was stay in bed and recover. This forced pause was incredibly challenging for someone who thrived on constant activity.

To make matters worse, some people involved in managing the GB Para Swim Team questioned Sarah's commitment, wondering if she was exaggerating her illness. Yet, Sarah's determination never wavered. After her six-week rest, she slowly started training again, building up from zero, determined to prove her critics wrong.

With grit and unwavering determination, Sarah made a full recovery. She began competing again, winning three gold medals at the World Championships in 2002. Her success sent a clear message to everyone who had doubted her capabilities.

However, Sarah's health struggles weren't over. In 2005, she suffered a persistent ear infection, and doctors warned her that swimming could lead to permanent hearing loss. They advised her to stay out of the pool indefinitely to allow her ears time to heal. Sarah was devastated but had learned not to dwell on things she couldn't control. Determined to stay fit, she started cycling and quickly discovered a new passion. She loved the thrill of racing around the velodrome and the challenge of pushing her limits on the bike. Cycling became more than just a way to stay in shape; it became her next great adventure and a new avenue for her incredible athletic talent.

British Cycling soon noticed her talent and invited her to a time trial. Sarah jumped at the chance, racing 12 laps and nearly breaking the world record. Everyone watching was stunned, staring at their stopwatches in disbelief. Sarah was offered a place on the GB Para-cycling team for the European Championships, which were only three weeks away. Determined to succeed, she spent the next three weeks learning everything she could about cycling, supported by her boyfriend, who was also part of the Para-cycling team. Sarah won three gold medals at the European Championships and broke a world record. In less than a year, she transitioned from champion swimmer to champion cyclist.

Sarah's achievements in cycling are nothing short of extraordinary. She won her first Paralympic gold medal in cycling at the 2008 Beijing Paralympics, setting a new world record. Over the years, she continued to dominate, winning multiple gold medals at the Paralympic Games in 2012, 2016 and 2020.

In 2022, Sarah had a serious crash in training and suffered concussion, broken ribs, and a partially collapsed lung. Her recovery was complicated by other illnesses including COVID-19 and a chest infection. Despite these setbacks, Sarah refused to contemplate retirement, determined to return to fitness and compete in her ninth Paralympic Games.

Sarah's hard work and determination paid off, and she traveled to Paris to compete in her ninth Paralympic Games, winning two more gold medals. With 19 gold medals (5 in swimming, 14 in cycling), she is Britain's most successful Paralympian. Over the years, Sarah has also won 38 Para-cycling world titles and is viewed as one of the greatest Para-cyclists of all time. Additionally, she is a six-time British national track champion in able-bodied events. Sarah's success in cycling shows what's possible with hard work, determination and a strong spirit.

In 2013, Sarah Storey was honored by the Queen and made a Dame Commander of the Order of the British Empire (DBE) for her achievements in Para-cycling. Being made a "Dame" in the UK is a major national award and one of the highest honors given to people who have made an extraordinary impact in their field.

Beyond her training, Sarah mentors other athletes and visits schools to share her inspirational story with the younger generation. She supports various charitable causes and often fundraises for breast cancer, inspired by her mother's diagnosis in 2004. Additionally, she works to raise the profile of Para-sport and campaigns for equal rights, urging the media to focus on athletes' performances rather than their disabilities. Sarah and her husband Barney have also founded Storey Racing - training and managing a team of 12 talented riders, helping each athlete reach their full potential.

We'll finish Sarah's story with part of a speech she gave to school children in 2021:

> *"Don't think, 'What if I had tried harder, done that extra practice session, gone that extra mile.' Never allow yourself to fail for want of practice and hard work."*

**Instances of Grit and Grace:**

**Grit**

- Her intensive swimming training whilst at school, waking up at 5 a.m. to do morning laps, and returning to the pool after school.
- Sarah's unwavering persistence in writing letters to the Paralympic swimming team organizers for 18 months, regularly updating them with her most recent swim times.
- Finding a plan B when the swimming coach at university refused to train her – organizing times when she could use the pool to train and later, commuting long distances to university whilst training at her home swimming club.
- Overcoming illnesses and injuries time and again to keep chasing her dreams.

*Grace*

- Acknowledging the role her friends and family have played in her success.
- Her work mentoring young athletes, supporting charitable causes, inspiring school children, and advocating for Para-sport.

*Key Life Lessons:*

- **Rise Above the Bullies:** Sarah faced bullying in school but used the negativity to fuel her drive to succeed. She focused on her swimming, demonstrating that the best way to deal with bullies is to rise above their hurtful words. Focus on your goals and remember that challenges are temporary. Seek support by talking to people who understand and believe in you. They can provide encouragement and perspective.
- **Always Look for Solutions to Challenges:** When the head coach at the university refused to train her, Sarah didn't give up. Instead, she found a way to train on her own, proving that there is always a way to overcome obstacles if you're determined to find a solution.
- **Be Open to Change**: Sarah's transition from swimming to cycling after a serious ear infection shows how being flexible can open doors to new opportunities.
- **Focus on What You Can Control:** Sarah couldn't control the actions of the bullies or the decisions of the university coach, but she could control how she responded. By choosing to stay positive and proactive, she found a way to overcome these challenges, build greater resilience, and keep working towards her goals.
- **Take Care of Yourself:** As Sarah discovered, proper nutrition and self-care are vital for peak performance. If you're struggling, reach out to someone you trust or seek guidance from a professional. You don't have to face challenges like this alone.

Sarah's journey is full of lessons on resilience and adaptability. Whether overcoming physical challenges, dealing with unsupportive people, or navigating personal issues, her story demonstrates that with courage and a problem-solving mindset, obstacles can become opportunities. Let her journey inspire you to face your challenges with courage, persistence, and the belief that you can achieve remarkable things.

Up next – an incredible journey with a skateboarding sensation whose passion and resilience have inspired girls and women worldwide.

# 13

# LETICIA BUFONI

"Anything you love, just follow your passion, follow your heart, and, you know, go out there. Don't let anyone tell you that you can't do it, just prove them wrong."

Leticia Bufoni

Picture this: a bustling neighborhood in São Paulo, Brazil, where the sound of skateboard wheels rolling over the pavement echoes through the streets. In the midst of this vibrant scene is Leticia Bufoni, a fearless young girl who discovered her passion for skateboarding when she was nine. Like perfecting a heel flip, Leticia's journey to becoming a world-class skateboarder required countless hours of practice, a few hard falls, and an unbreakable spirit. Join Leticia as she carves her own path, proving that with grit and determination, you can ride the ramps of life and soar to incredible heights.

Leticia was born in Brazil on April 13, 1993. From an early age, she loved playing football in the street with the local boys and dreamt of becoming a professional player. She was often called a tomboy, but the label never bothered her—she was having too much fun. However, a few years later, everything changed. Her friends stopped playing soccer and started skateboarding. Without anyone to play soccer with, she decided to give skateboarding a try. It wasn't long before Leticia was captivated by the local skateboarders, their impressive skills, and the amazing tricks they could perform. Watching them lit a fire in her soul; she was determined to learn and perfect those moves. Leticia spent endless hours practicing, holding onto the gate of her house, trying over and over again to master new tricks. *"I fell in love and just got addicted,"* she says. She was determined to outperform and impress the boys, hoping one day they would accept her into their group.

However, there was one big problem: Leticia was the only girl in her neighborhood who liked to skate. While most of her family supported her, Leticia's father disapproved of his daughter skateboarding; he thought it was a sport for boys and bums. He wanted her to focus on her schoolwork and hang out with girls. One day, he saw Leticia skateboarding with about ten boys and was furious. He grabbed a saw and broke her skateboard in half, hoping to make her stop. Leticia was heartbroken, but she wasn't going to give up. The next day, she asked friends for spare skateboard parts and built herself a new board. She told her dad she loved skateboarding too much to quit. After that, her father relented and allowed Leticia to keep skating. He still didn't like it but understood that taking her board away would only make her want to skate even more.

When Leticia was 11, she entered her first skateboarding contest. Her father wasn't keen, but a friend persuaded him to let her participate. Reluctantly, he agreed and took her to the contest. Watching her skate, he realized how good she was. He saw her potential and noticed other girls skating, too. From that day on, he became her biggest supporter. He took her to contests and skateparks so she could practice and improve.

Not long after, a friend gave Leticia a DVD showing girls skateboarding in the United States. Watching the footage made her eyes sparkle with excitement. She realized that women's skateboarding was popular in other countries, and if she worked hard, she could become a professional skateboarder.

When Leticia was 14, she was invited to Los Angeles to participate in the X Games, an annual event showcasing the world's best skateboarders. Leticia was ecstatic; it was the break she had been dreaming of. However, her Brazilian sponsors didn't want her to go—they thought she was too young and refused to fund her trip. With the family unable to afford the trip, Leticia and her father, now her biggest fan, worked together to find a company willing to sponsor their journey to the US.

On arriving in Los Angeles, Leticia quickly fell in love with the American skate scene. She came eighth in her first X Games and secured several small sponsors. Leticia realized she would need to stay in the States to pursue her dream of becoming a professional skateboarder. Convincing her dad to let her remain in the US with friends when he went back to Brazil was a significant challenge, as she was only 14. Her father eventually made a deal with her: If she could successfully land an ollie inward heel flip, a difficult trick, he would let her stay. She practiced relentlessly and nailed it!

When her father returned to Brazil, Leticia stayed in LA. Initially, she found it tough—being alone in a new country, trying to settle in, learn a new language, and make friends. As a girl in a male-dominated sport, finding good sponsorship deals was hard, and the level of competition was much higher than in Brazil.

For four long years, Leticia trained and competed without securing a top spot. Broken bones and fractures became part of her story, but they never broke her spirit. Despite the setbacks, Leticia never lost hope. She continued training and practicing - every fall and every injury taught her something, bringing her one step closer to her dream.

Fast forward to 2015, a year of significant highs and lows for Leticia. She agreed to do a feature for a popular magazine celebrating incredible male and female athletes. The photo shoot showcased athletes in minimal clothing, highlighting their strength, muscles, and the results of their hard training and healthy eating habits. Leticia was thrilled to be asked. However, the media criticized her for participating. They suggested she had lost interest in skateboarding and was more interested in fitness and fashion modeling. Leticia was shocked and upset; this simply wasn't true. She had sacrificed so much for skateboarding and worked so hard; she couldn't believe people could be so cruel.

Leticia refused to let the negativity discourage her. Instead, she used it as motivation to push harder and skate better. Later that year, she clinched victory at the Street League Super Crown Women's Final. This win boosted her confidence and proved to her critics that she had the skills, courage, and resilience to be a champion. It is a powerful reminder that success often follows hard and challenging times.

Leticia Bufoni's journey to the Tokyo Olympics was an uphill battle. With skateboarding making its Olympic debut, Leticia was determined to participate. Representing Brazil would be a dream come true. However, nothing could have prepared her for what happened next.

During training, she damaged a ligament in her ankle and had to take time off to recover. After some rest, she went to China to compete in a qualifying event for the Olympics but injured her foot again before the main competition started. She was in a lot of pain and considered pulling out but decided to compete anyway. With grit, courage, and determination, she pulled off some incredible tricks and won the event, bringing her one step closer to fulfilling her Olympic dream.

However, winning came at a price. Her foot was in bad shape and needed 60 days of rest to heal. With the clock ticking for Olympic qualifications, she couldn't afford to sit out for too long. Leticia bravely returned to competition earlier than planned, desperate for the points she needed to keep her Olympic dream alive. But then, disaster struck: She broke her foot again. Leticia felt her Olympic dream slipping away; she was devastated and didn't want to see or talk to anyone.

Leticia soon realized that feeling sorry for herself wouldn't help her achieve her dreams. Deep down, she knew she had to keep trying. She started physiotherapy again and worked hard to get back on track. Her unwavering spirit and determination shone brightly. Then, something unexpected happened—the Olympics were postponed due to COVID-19. For Leticia, this was a silver lining; she now had time to recover fully.

Tokyo 2020: With her impressive skateboarding skills and trailblazing spirit, Leticia was one of the favorites to win an Olympic medal. However, things didn't go as planned. Another competitor pulled off amazing tricks in the last rounds, and Leticia didn't qualify for the Olympic final. Unfortunately, despite our best efforts, life doesn't always go the way we plan. Leticia was disappointed to miss out on a place in the final but overjoyed when her Brazilian teammate Rayssa Leal won the silver medal.

Some years earlier, Rayssa had mentioned that Leticia was her biggest inspiration and role model. Soon after, Leticia began mentoring the young skateboarding superstar. They became good friends, and Leticia cheered wildly from the stands as Rayssa performed incredible tricks to win the silver medal.

Leticia has faced some serious slams in her skateboarding journey. From gnarly wipeouts to painful spills, she's experienced it all. One of her worst injuries was during a competition in 2014. She was in second place with one round to go. It was crunch time; she knew she needed to pull off something big to clinch the win. So, she went for a lipslide but took a massive slam instead. When she woke up, she was in an ambulance on the way to hospital. Her hip was broken, she had a concussion, and her face was black and blue from bruising. But every time she fell, Leticia was determined to get back up and skate again as soon as she could. Broken bones and bruises didn't stop her; they were just part of the ride. Leticia's resilience shows that even the toughest falls can't keep a true skater down.

Leticia is a six-time X Games Gold Medallist, with 12 Summer X Games medals, making her the most decorated female Summer X Games athlete. She's an SLS Super Crown champion and a five-time Guinness World Record holder. Leticia was Brazil's Female Skater of the Year in 2009 and 2010, and in 2018, she was named one of the 'Most Powerful Women in International Sports.' Leticia has won or been featured on many other award shortlists. She is also a character in a skateboarding video game!

Despite her incredible success and the growing popularity of women's skateboarding, men's skateboarding still receives much more attention and support. Leticia is determined to change this. She actively supports and inspires young female skateboarders, using her skills and fame to raise the profile of women's skateboarding worldwide. She's been involved in some crazy projects, including doing a kickflip over a dinosaur at the Natural History Museum in London and skateboarding out of a plane into a skydive! Leticia also works with *Boarding for Breast Cancer* to raise awareness of the disease, promote healthy eating, and support those affected.

### *Instances of Grit and Grace:*

### *Grit*

- Refusing to give up on her dream of becoming a professional skateboarder when other local girls lost interest in the sport.
- Her resolve to keep skating despite opposition from her father.

- Her early years in LA, feeling homesick and competing for four years without securing a top spot.
- Her determination to compete in a qualifying event for the Olympics despite being in pain after injuring her foot.
- Always getting back on her skateboard after taking some serious slams.

*Grace*

- Her joy when Brazilian teammate and friend Rayssa Leal won the silver medal at the Olympics.
- Her work supporting and mentoring young female skateboarders – inspiring them to chase their dreams and believe in their potential.
- Leticia has spoken out about the negative remarks made by some girls in the skateboarding community, advocating for a more supportive and encouraging environment among girls in the sport.

*Key Life Lessons:*

- **Get Back Up After Falls:** You might not be looking to become a professional skateboarder, but the principle remains the same. Whatever your passion—be it sports, arts, science, or something else—the road will be tough. There will be setbacks. You might face obstacles that make you question whether it's all worth it. Sometimes, like Leticia, you may take a few hard falls that knock you down. But falling doesn't mean you've failed. Every fall is a chance to learn and grow stronger. The most important thing is to get back up, think about how you can improve, and try again.
- **Follow Your Passion:** Whether it's playing football, skateboarding, painting, or coding, find what you love and pursue it wholeheartedly. In Leticia's words: *"What I always say is, if you love something, if it's your passion, just go for it.*

*Don't let anyone say you can't do it, and just follow your dreams."*
- **Work Hard:** Success doesn't come overnight. Just like Leticia, you need to put in the hours, practice relentlessly, and be prepared to face setbacks. Hard work is crucial for turning dreams into reality.
- **Seek Inspiration:** Just as seeing other girls skateboarding in the US opened Leticia's eyes to new possibilities, Leticia became a role model for Rayssa Leal. Always seek role models and inspiration to fuel your journey.

Leticia Bufoni's story is a powerful reminder that chasing your dreams is always worth it. Even if others don't understand or support you initially, you can work to convince them over time. Whatever your dream is—skateboarding, acting, science, or anything else—hold onto it tightly. Work hard, believe in yourself, and never give up.

Now, we're off to the beautiful beaches of Hawaii to meet a surfer who didn't just ride the waves but also rose above a life-changing challenge. Get ready to be swept away by her incredible journey and unbreakable spirit.

## 14

# BETHANY HAMILTON

"Courage doesn't mean you don't get afraid. Courage means you don't let fear stop you."

Bethany Hamilton

We couldn't finish this book without including Bethany Hamilton's extraordinary story. You may have heard of her before—her journey is one of the most inspiring and uplifting you'll ever come across.

Imagine being 13 years old, living in beautiful Hawaii, with a love for surfing as deep as the ocean. You spend your days surfing new waves with friends and family. That was Bethany Hamilton's life—until everything changed in an instant. On a calm October morning, while riding the waves with her best friend, Bethany was attacked by a shark. In the blink of an eye, she found herself fighting for her life. She lost her left arm, and it seemed her dream of becoming a professional surfer might be over. But this wasn't where her story ended; it's where it truly began.

Bethany Meilani Hamilton was born on February 8, 1990, in Lihue, Kauai, Hawaii. Raised in a family of avid surfers, she was destined to fall in love with the ocean. Her parents, both surfers, introduced her to the waves at a young age. By eight, she was already competing in surfing competitions, eager to keep up with her two older brothers and surf the bigger waves like they did. With her natural talent and fierce determination, Bethany quickly made a name for herself in the surfing community and earned her first sponsorship when she was nine.

On October 31, 2003, Bethany was surfing at Tunnels Beach in Ha'ena with her best friend Alana, Alana's dad, and Alana's brother. It was a day like any other, filled with the promise of catching some good waves; they were all waiting for the perfect wave to come rolling in. Suddenly, out of nowhere, Bethany was attacked by a 14-foot tiger shark, which severed her left arm close to the shoulder. One moment, she was anticipating the thrill of riding a wave; the next, she was fighting for her life. Alana's dad quickly tied his surfboard leash around Bethany's arm to prevent excessive blood loss, and she was rushed to the hospital, where she underwent life-saving surgery.

The immediate aftermath was understandably traumatic. Bethany spent five days in hospital recovering and coming to terms with her new reality, surrounded by her family and friends. Her mom encouraged her to be thankful she was alive and reassured her that, despite how impossible it seemed, good would come from her accident.

Bethany realized that her life would be very different in the future, but her mom's words planted seeds of hope. Instead of wallowing in sorrow, she chose to be grateful for simply being alive. While in hospital, one of her brother's friends visited her. He had lost a leg while surfing a few years earlier but had learned to surf again. Hearing his story, Bethany's eyes lit up; she realized that surfing with one arm was entirely possible.

This visit gave her hope and a chance to dream again. Surfing wasn't just a hobby for Bethany; it was her passion, her love. Losing an arm meant facing new challenges, but her love for surfing was greater than her fear of sharks. She decided then and there that she would at least try to get back on her board.

*"I didn't wake up in the hospital thinking I was invincible and was gonna get back to surfing. After getting a hint of inspiration, I had to dream it up, flip my mindset, and be willing to do what I had not seen anyone else do. This was a challenge to live in faith."*

Just four weeks after the attack, Bethany was back on her surfboard. Supported by friends and family, her first few attempts were challenging—she couldn't get up on the board like she used to. Her father suggested a new technique to help her find her balance. She tried it, and it worked. Riding that first wave back to shore brought a feeling of pure joy, a surge of hope vital to her healing process.

Bethany's faith in God was a fundamental part of her healing and accepting what had happened. Drawing strength from her spiritual beliefs, Bethany chose to believe that God had a plan for her, even if it wasn't clear to her at the time. This faith provided her with inner strength and a sense of peace that helped her face the challenges ahead.

Riding that first wave after her accident was a huge thrill for Bethany, but her first few months back in the water were tough. Her dad modified her surfboard to make it easier and safer for her. Learning to balance on the board again was difficult, and she had to find new ways to surf with only one arm. It took hours of practice, falls, and failures, but she never gave up. Throughout, she was supported by her family, friends, community, and strong Christian faith.

As well as recovering from the physical and emotional scars of the shark attack, Bethany faced another challenge. Practically overnight, she went from being a talented young surfer to a global sensation, with her story making headlines worldwide. Journalists from around the globe flocked to Hawaii, eager to capture her story. For a young girl from a small town coping with the aftermath of a life-threatening shark attack and learning to live with one arm, the attention was overwhelming.

However, letters soon started pouring in from children who saw her as an inspiration. These heartfelt messages revealed how much her story was helping others overcome their own challenges and recover from their injuries. Bethany realized she had a greater role to play and made it her mission to share her journey with an even wider audience.

Her achievements after losing her arm are nothing short of extraordinary. Just two months after returning to the waves, Bethany entered her first competition and placed fifth. The following year, she won two regional competitions. She didn't stop there; she went on to compete in professional surfing events worldwide, winning some and placing high in others, ultimately earning a spot in the Surfer's Hall of Fame in 2017. Additionally, she has tow surfed some of the biggest waves in Hawaii and was the first woman to compete in a specialty barrel-riding event in Indonesia. She is truly unstoppable! At the heart of Bethany's incredible achievements lies her belief:

*"People can do whatever they want if they just set their heart to it, and just never give up, and just go out there and do it."*

Bethany's story is a shining example of hope and resilience, earning her the ESPY Award for Best Comeback Athlete and the Courage Teen Choice Award in 2004. Her autobiography, "Soul Surfer," which details her ordeal and comeback, became a bestseller and was later adapted into a feature film of the same name in 2011. The movie brought her story to an even wider audience, highlighting her faith and perseverance.

Beyond her surfing career, Bethany is a motivational speaker, sharing her story worldwide and encouraging people to overcome difficulties with faith, determination, and hope. In 2007, she founded the Beautifully Flawed Foundation, a nonprofit organization supporting shark attack survivors and amputees worldwide. More recently, she launched an online course, "Unstoppable Life," to inspire and empower girls to live fulfilling and meaningful lives.

*Instances of Grit and Grace:*

*Grit*

- Facing her fears head-on, returning to the ocean just one month after losing her arm.
- Her determination - not only to surf again but to excel and compete at the highest levels.

*Grace*

- Choosing to accept her injury as part of her life's journey and share her story to inspire and motivate others facing challenges.
- Founding her nonprofit organization to support shark attack survivors and amputees worldwide.
- Her gratitude to her family and friends for their ongoing support and encouragement.

*Key Life Lessons:*

- **Look for Silver Linings:** Whatever the obstacle, however big the setback, there's always something to be grateful for. Even in the days immediately following the shark attack, Bethany's mother encouraged her to be thankful she was alive.

- **Always Have the Courage to Try**: Bethany got back on her surfboard after the shark attack, not knowing if she'd be able to surf again. The important thing is she had the courage to try. As Bethany wrote in a social media post 20 years later: *"When you have your 'Shark Attack' moments in life, I hope you're willing to try and give life your best shot! You too CAN OVERCOME!"*
- **You Control Your Response to Challenges:** Bethany's story serves as a poignant reminder that life can throw unexpected challenges our way. However, it's how we respond to these challenges that defines us. Just as Bethany refused to let the shark attack stop her surfing, we can refuse to let hurdles and obstacles stop us from achieving our dreams.
- **Surround Yourself with Supportive People:** Bethany's family, friends, and community supported her recovery and return to surfing. Surround yourself with people who believe in you and lift you up. Whether it's family, friends, or mentors, having a strong support system can provide the encouragement and strength needed to face life's biggest challenges.

Bethany Hamilton's journey isn't just about a surfer girl who survived a shark attack; it's a story relevant to anyone facing struggles and challenges. Whether it's school, friendships, or personal goals, everyone has obstacles to overcome. Her experience teaches us that even the most daunting obstacles can be conquered if you face your fears, lean on your support systems, and stay committed to your passions.

As you navigate your own life's waves, remember Bethany's journey. With the right mindset and support, there's no limit to what you can achieve. Keep pushing forward and riding your own waves.

# CONCLUSION

As we turn the final pages of this book, I feel like I should be in the stands, cheering loudly for these amazing women and their incredible achievements. These women are champions not only in sports but also in life, showing both grit and grace on their journeys.

Each of these incredible athletes faced challenges, setbacks, and hurdles that could have stopped them in their tracks. But instead of giving up, they used those obstacles as stepping stones to greatness. From soccer fields to swimming pools, from gymnastics arenas to tennis courts, these women have shown the world what it means to dream big, work hard, and never give up. I hope their stories light a spark within you.

These remarkable women did more than just excel in their sports; they broke barriers and challenged stereotypes, paving the way for future generations. By daring to compete in areas once dominated by men or pushing the boundaries within their sports, they opened doors and expanded possibilities for girls everywhere. Today, thanks to their courage and determination, girls have more opportunities than ever before to play, compete, and excel in any sport.

Remember each story, not just for the medals and trophies but for the spirit, determination, and courage shown by each athlete. They were once girls just like you, with dreams that may have seemed out of reach—until they reached a little further. Each chapter has revealed that success is not only about how fast you run or how high you jump but about how bravely you pursue your goals, how persistently you work to overcome obstacles, how gracefully you learn from setbacks, and how kindly you treat others.

This book celebrates women who have reached incredible heights in sport, but its message goes much further: every girl can achieve their dreams. So, what's your dream? Is it to score the winning goal? Swim faster than anyone else? Write a bestselling novel? Become an award-winning actor? Or perhaps invent something that changes the world? Whatever your dream is, believe it is possible. You have what it takes to do something amazing. So, find what you love, set goals, challenge yourself, and find ways to overcome any obstacles that come your way. And don't forget to have fun!

It's time to follow your dreams with grit and grace…

# One Last Thing...

Thank you for taking the time to read "Inspiring True Stories for Girls - Sports Edition".

Before I go, I wanted to share one last quote with you:

> "Every woman's success should be an inspiration to another. We're strongest when we cheer each other on."
>
> — Serena Williams

This book has been all about celebrating that spirit.

I hope these stories have left you feeling inspired and ready to chase your own dreams, or have at least got you thinking about what might be possible...

By leaving a review, you could help other girls find these awesome stories, and inspire them to believe in themselves, go after their dreams, and keep cheering each other on.

Let's spread that girl power together!

It's really quick and easy to write a review - just scan the QR code below to go directly to the Amazon review page:

*Thank you so much*
*Stella xx*

# Girls with Grit and Grace

**INSPIRATION AND EMPOWERMENT BUNDLE**

Want to keep feeling inspired and unstoppable?

Or need a little extra motivation?

Head over to our website and grab your FREE Inspiration and Empowerment Bundle! It's packed with awesome stuff—like inspiring quotes to fire you up, fun activities to help you dream big, and creative challenges like making your own vision board or writing a letter to your future self.

It's your ultimate guide to dreaming big, setting goals, and having fun along the way.

Go check it out and start planning your amazing future right now!

Just scan the QR code or visit: www.girlswithgritandgrace.com

# GLOSSARY

ACC: Atlantic Coast Conference (an organization that brings together top colleges on the East Coast of US)

CWHL: Canadian Women's Hockey League

Grand Slam: The four big, most prestigious tennis tournaments (the Australian Open, the French Open, Wimbledon, and the US Open)

IIHF: International Ice Hockey Federation

LPGA: Ladies Professional Golf Association

MVP: Most Valuable Player

NBA: National Basketball Association

NCAA: National Collegiate Athletics Association

NHL: National Hockey League

PGA: Professional Golf Association

UEFA: The Union of European Football Associations

WNBA: Women's National Basketball Association

WPS: Women's Professional Soccer

WUSA: Women's United Soccer Association

# ABOUT THE AUTHOR

*"While we've come a long way, the incredible successes of women are still often overshadowed by the achievements of men.*

*Through my books, I hope to shine a brighter light on some incredible women who never gave up, inspiring girls to believe that with hard work and resilience, they can achieve anything they set their minds to."*

Stella Bright

Stella Bright is mother to three children, a son and two teenage daughters. She lives in England with her husband, children and flat coated retriever.

Having lacked confidence growing up, Stella is always looking for ways to inspire her children and young people everywhere to believe in themselves and have the courage to chase their dreams.

# REFERENCES / FURTHER READING / LISTENING

## VENUS AND SERENA WILLIAMS

Buchholz, L. (2022, August 12). *The philanthropic ventures of Serena Williams*. March8. https://march8.com/articles/the-philanthropic-ventures-of-serena-williams

Corbett, M. L. (2015, July 28). *The biggest obstacles Serena Williams faces in quest for calendar slam*. Bleacher Report. https://bleacherreport.com/articles/2530185-the-biggest-obstacles-serena-williams-faces-in-quest-for-calendar-slam

Davis, S., & Gopal, T. (2022, August 13). *Serena Williams became the greatest tennis player of all-time even as she endured racist and sexist attacks in the media*. Insider. https://www.insider.com/serena-williams-endured-racism-sexism-media-throughout-career-2022-8

Dregni, M. (2024, March 14). *Venus Williams on setbacks, comebacks, and resilience*. Experience Life. https://experiencelife.lifetime.life/article/venus-williams-on-setbacks-comebacks-and-resilience/

Greatness Authors. (2023, January 2021). *What Serena & Venus Williams have to teach us about overcoming adversity*. Greatness. https://greatness.com/what-serena-venus-williams-have-to-teach-us-about-overcoming-adversity

*Serena Williams*. (2019, March 11). Wikipedia. https://en.wikipedia.org/wiki/Serena_Williams

The Editors of Encyclopedia Britannica. (2024, January 25). *Serena Williams*. Britannica. https://www.britannica.com/biography/Serena-Williams

Venus Williams. (2024a, August 4). *Wikipedia* https://en.wikipedia.org/wiki/Venus_Williams

Wildcat0206. (2022, November 9). *A look back at Serena Williams' biggest achievements*. The Grandstand. https://tenngrand.com/a-look-back-at-serena-williams-biggest-achievements-following-her-retirement/

## MARTA VIEIRA DA SILVA

Augustyn, A. (2019). *Marta*. Britannica. https://www.britannica.com/biography/Marta

da Silva, M. (2017). *Letter to my younger self*. The Players' Tribune. https://www.theplayerstribune.com/articles/marta-brazil-letter-to-my-younger-self

National Football Museum. (n.d.). *Meet Marta: The Record-Breaking Brazilian Football Player*. Google Arts & Culture. https://artsandculture.google.com/story/meet-marta-the-record-breaking-brazilian-football-player/UAWxrX7MR4XIfg?hl=en

Prescott, L. (2019, July 16). *How Marta inspired a revolution in women's football both on and off the pitch*. These Football Times. https://thesefootballtimes.co/2019/07/17/how-marta-inspired-a-revolution-in-womens-football-both-on-and-off-the-pitch/

Simplicio, R. (n.d.). The queen of football. Goal. https://www.goal.com/story/queen-of-

football-marta/index.html
UN Women (n.d.). *UN Women Goodwill Ambassador for women and girls in sport Marta Vieira da Silva.* https://www.unwomen.org/en/partnerships/goodwill-ambassadors/marta-vieira-da-silva

## LINDSEY VONN

After-School All-Stars. (2023, March 16). *Lindsey Vonn joins national board of directors.* Afterschoolallstars.org.https://afterschoolallstars.org/lindseyvonn/#:~:text=She

Bried, E. (2014, February 20). *Lindsey Vonn: How to be fearless.* Self. https://www.self.com/story/lindsey-vonn-fearless-tips

Cohen, J. (2024, January 16). *Lindsey Vonn: Lessons learned from Olympic champion + ski legend.* (#311) [Audio Podcast Episode]. *Habits & Hustle.* https://podcasts.apple.com/us/podcast/episode-311-lindsey-vonn-lessons-learned-from-olympic/id1451897026?i=1000641805749

EW Staff. (2022, January 21). *Lindsey Vonn on how a childhood meeting with Picabo Street changed her life.* Entertainment Weekly. https://ew.com/books/lindsay-vonn-rise-bold-school/#:~:text=%22Picabo%20Street%20was%20my%20idol

*Lindsey Vonn.* (2021, September 13). Wikipedia. https://en.wikipedia.org/wiki/Lindsey_Vonn

*Lindsey Vonn quotes.* (n.d.). Brainy Quote. https://www.brainyquote.com/authors/lindsey-vonn-quotes

Scipioni, J. (2021, October 21). *Lindsey Vonn spent her 19-year career battling depression—here are the tactics she used to stay at the top.* CNBC. https://www.cnbc.com/2021/10/21/ex-skier-lindsey-vonn-on-success-habits-and-living-with-depression.html

Woodruff, J. (2022, January 28). *Olympian skier Lindsey Vonn on what drove her success, and the "heavy price" of her career.* PBS NewsHour. https://www.pbs.org/newshour/show/olympian-skier-lindsey-vonn-on-what-drove-her-success-and-the-heavy-price-of-her-career

## HAYLEY WICKENHEISER

Belknap, C. & Telfer N. (Hosts) (2020, October 22). *Changing the Culture of Hockey with Hayley Wickenheiser* (S9 E42) [Audio podcast episode] In *Cat & Nat Unfiltered.* https://catandnat.ca/new-blog/2020/10/1/changing-the-culture-of-hockey-with-hayley-wickenheiser

Dickenson, A. (Host) (2020, July 8). *Hayley Wickenheiser | Four-time Olympic gold medalist* (#4) [Audio podcast episode] *Reinvention.* Buzzsprout. https://reinventionpodcast.buzzsprout.com/1155911/4482065-episode-4-hayley-wickenheiser-four-time-olympic-gold-medalist-director-of-player-development-toronto-maple-leafs

Freeborn, J. (2013, September 18). *Hayley Wickenheiser.* (2018). The Canadian Encyclopedia. https://www.thecanadianencyclopedia.ca/en/article/hayley-wickenheiser

*Hayley Wickenheiser.* (2021, February 24). Wikipedia. https://en.wikipedia.org/wiki/Hayley_Wickenheiser

Jay, M. (2019, November 19). *Hayley Wickenheiser inducted into Hockey Hall of Fame.*

The Ice Garden. https://www.theicegarden.com/hayley-wickenheiser-inducted-into-hockey-hall-of-fame-speech/
McLeod, K. (2020, March 2). *Getting back in the game*. UHN Foundation. https://uhnfoundation.ca/stories/getting-back-in-the-game/
Rutherford, K. *(n.d.). Hayley Wickenheiser on her unmatched career, and life after hockey.* Sportsnet. https://www.sportsnet.ca/hockey/nhl/hayley-wickenheiser-unmatched-career-life-hockey/
Wickenheiser, H. (2021, October 10). Life lessons from Canadian hockey great Hayley Wickenheiser. *The Globe and Mail*. https://www.theglobeandmail.com/sports/hockey/article-hayley-wickenheiser-shares-life-lessons-from-the-ice-in-her-new-book/

## TAMIKA CATCHINGS

Benbow, D. H. (2016, September 17). *Tamika Catchings: A reluctant superstar*. Indy Star. https://eu.indystar.com/story/sports/basketball/wnba/fever/2016/09/17/tamika-catchings-reluctant-superstar/86233128/
*Catchings, Tamika 1979– | Encyclopedia.com*. (n.d.) https://www.encyclopedia.com/education/news-wires-white-papers-and-books/catchings-tamika-1979
Illini Land FCA. (2016, April 28). *Tamika Catchings - Illini Land FCA keynote Speaker* [Video]. YouTube. https://www.youtube.com/watch?v=djSs5bNTlyY
Quinlan, E. (2022, October 31). *Be B.O.L.D.: Tamika Catchings encourages FFA members*. AgriNews. https://www.agrinews-pubs.com/features/2022/10/31/be-bold-tamika-catchings-encourages-ffa-members/
Spalding, J. (2016, August 8). *Tamika Catchings's last shot*. Indianapolis Monthly. https://www.indianapolismonthly.com/arts-and-culture/sports/tamika-catchings-last-shot/
speakinc. (2023, March 7). *Tamika Catchings | Keynote Speaker | SpeakInc* [Video]. YouTube. https://www.youtube.com/watch?v=Ad6Ae9Rc9tc
*Tamika Catchings: a Two-State All-Time great in high school hoops*. (n.d.). https://www.nfhs.org/articles/tamika-catchings-a-two-state-all-time-great-in-high-school-hoops/

## ANNIKA SÖRENSTAM

ABC News. (2003, May 14). *Sorenstam's golf plans stirs controversy*. https://abcnews.go.com/GMA/story?id=125165&page=1
*Annika Sörenstam*. (2023, December 8). Wikipedia. https://en.wikipedia.org/wiki/Annika_S%C3%B6renstam
*BiO | LPGA | Ladies Professional Golf Association*. (n.d.). LPGA. https://www.lpga.com/players/annika-sorenstam/81956/bio
Hurlburt, B. (Host) (2021, May 18). *How a shy girl grew up to not fear excellence (#15)*. [Audio Podcast Episode] Spotify. https://open.spotify.com/episode/7nWOUCO8gfZRBCrVHrYolt

Gilleece, D. (2003, May 18). *Invading a man's world*. Irish Independent. https://www.independent.ie/sport/invading-a-mans-world/26231598.html

Jessop, A. (2015, September 21). *Hall of fame golfer Annika Sorentstam uses lessons learned on the course to succeed in business*. HuffPost. https://www.huffpost.com/entry/hall-of-fame-golfer-annik_b_8159286

Mindbodygreen. (2021, May 7). *How to be a winner | Annika Sörenstam, all-time greatest professional female golfer*. Apple Podcasts. https://podcasts.apple.com/no/podcast/how-to-be-winner-annika-s%C3%B6renstam-all-time-greatest/id1246494475?i=1000520603042

Natacha. (2019, August 6). *Exclusive Interview with Golf Legend Annika Sorenstam*. Futuri Visio. https://golfscape.com/blog/exclusive-interview-annika-sorenstam/

No Laying Up. (2019, January 20). *189 – Annika Sörenstam*. Apple Podcasts. https://podcasts.apple.com/gb/podcast/nlu-podcast-episode-189-annika-s%C3%B6renstam/id880837011?i=1000428072677

*There are Going to be Hurdles in Every Journey, But You Will be*. (n.d.). https://theannika.com/news/there-are-going-to-be-hurdles-in-every-journey-but-you-will-be

Wallace, R. (2024, May 3). *The evolution of Annika*. Global Golf Post. https://www.globalgolfpost.com/featured/the-evolution-of-annika/

## SIMONE BILES

Baer, S. K. (2021, August 21). *Simone Biles said she would probably have been "too stubborn" earlier in her career to prioritize her mental health*. BuzzFeed News. https://www.buzzfeednews.com/article/skbaer/simone-biles-biden-mental-health-olympics

Barbaro, M. (Host) (2021, July 30). *The story of Simone Biles*. [Audio podcast episode] The Daily https://podcasts.apple.com/us/podcast/the-story-of-simone-biles/id1200361736?i=1000530497320

Brodsky, S. (2024, June 27). *5 gymnastics moves named after Simone Biles*. Popsugar. https://www.popsugar.com/fitness/gymnastics-moves-named-after-simone-biles-46488523

Capatides, C. (2018, February 2). *Simone Biles extends helping hand to other U.S. foster kids*. CBS News. https://www.cbsnews.com/news/simone-biles-extends-helping-hand-to-other-u-s-foster-kids/

Kohler, L. (2021, July 30). *4 lessons employers can learn from Simone Biles*. Forbes. https://www.forbes.com/sites/lindsaykohler/2021/07/30/4-lessons-employers-can-learn-from-simone-biles/?sh=53961b907695

Quinn, D. (2016, November 16). *Simone Biles recounts tearful moment when a coach called her 'Fat'* Peoplemag. https://people.com/health/simone-biles-today-fat/

Sidmore-Williams, A. & Siffrinn, B. (Hosts) (2021 July 28). *Simone Biles turns the Olympics upside down*. (#31). [Audio podcast episode] *Rich and Daily* https://podcasts.apple.com/lu/podcast/simone-biles-turns-the-olympics-upside-down/id1571355127?i=1000530322816

*Simone Biles Rising | Netflix Official site*. (n.d.). https://www.netflix.com/gb/title/81700902

Stand Together. (n.d.). *Simone Biles goes above and beyond for foster kids*. https://stand together.org/news/simone-biles-works-with-friends-of-the-children-to-advocate-for-foster-kids/

Stone, C. (2016, November 17). Simone Biles opens up about being body shamed by a coach. *Glamour*. https://www.glamour.com/story/simone-biles-body-shaming

Thomas, H. (n.d.). *7 lessons learned from Simone Biles at the Tokyo Olympics*. Pinnacle Gymnastics. https://blog.pinngym.com/lessons-learned-from-simone-biles-at-the-tokyo-olympics

## DEEDEE TROTTER

Deedee Trotter. (2020, May 23). *Amazing commencement speech for 2020 graduates! from Olympic champion DeeDee Trotter* [Video]. YouTube. https://www.youtube.com/watch?v=6CCynLlwo5c

Radvillas, H. (2020, December 15). DeeDee Trotter talks teamwork. *TrueSport*. https://truesport.org/teamwork/deedee-trotter-talks-teamwork/

*Sample video for DeeDee Trotter*. (n.d.). [Video]. Key Speakers Bureau. https://keyspeakers.com/bio.php?5436-deedee-trotter

speakinc. (2023a, March 7). *DeeDee Trotter | Keynote Speaker | SpeakInc* [Video]. YouTube. https://www.youtube.com/watch?v=2V0ABrUUe1o

Wharton, P. (2023, January 4) *I Can, I Must, I Will with Three Time Olympic Medallist DeeDee Trotter (S4, E9)*. [Audio Podcast Episode]. *Intrinsic Drive*. https://podcasts.apple.com/us/podcast/i-can-i-must-i-will-with-three-time-olympic-medalist/id1563963162?i=1000592339619

## KATIE LEDECKY

Auerbach, N. (2021, May 26) *Katie Ledecky vs. Herself*. NY Times. https://theathletic.com/2609313/2021/05/26/katie-ledecky-olympics-tokyo-swimming/

Charboneau, M. (2024, August 7). Katie Ledecky. *Biography*. https://www.biography.com/athletes/katie-ledecky

Fares Ksebati. (2021, July 26). How Katie Ledecky became a swimming LEGEND [Video] YouTube. https://www.youtube.com/watch?v=5hQ8ivBqWQM

Glock, A. (2018, December 10). Dominant 20 -- Katie Ledecky on her swimming origins, breaking records and her one fear ESPN. *ESPN.com*. https://www.espn.com/espnw/voices/story/_/id/25499475/dominant-20-katie-ledecky-swimming-origins-breaking-records-one-fear

*Katie Ledecky on never losing the fun from when she first began swimming*. (2021, August 20). Adidas News Site | Press Resources for All Brands, Sports and Innovations. https://news.adidas.com/swimming/katie-ledecky-on-never-losing-the-fun-from-when-she-first-began-swimming/s/a974c0b0-b302-4b02-b8f7-eb9df5cb88d9

*Katie Ledecky*. (2024, August 6) Wikipedia. https://en.wikipedia.org/wiki/Katie_Ledecky

Palace, K. & Parker, M. (2022, October 10). *10 Lessons Katie Ledecky teaches us (# 175)*. Champion's Mojo. https://www.championsmojo.com/10-lessons-katie-ledecky-teaches-us-episode-175/

PBS NewsHour. (2016, August 25). *At the pool with freestyle phenom Katie Ledecky* [Video]. YouTube. https://www.youtube.com/watch?v=bOmFLE6gtHg

Reider, D. (2021, September 23). *Katie Ledecky embraces challenges to come in her new Gator chapter*. Swimming World News. https://www.swimmingworldmagazine.com/news/katie-ledecky-embraces-challenges-to-come-in-her-new-gator-chapter/

Sullivan, R. (2016, March 31). *What's Katie Ledecky's secret?* Vogue. https://www.vogue.com/article/katie-ledecky-freestyle-swimmer-olympics-2016-rio-de-janeiro-team-usa

Swimming World. (2022, October 6). *Katie Ledecky receives Athletes for Hope Community Hero Award*. Swimming World News. https://www.swimmingworldmagazine.com/news/katie-ledecky-receives-athletes-for-hope-community-hero-award/

Woodfruff, J. (2021, August 17). *Katie Ledecky on her Tokyo wins, mental health and gender equality in sports*. PBS NewsHour. https://www.pbs.org/newshour/show/katie-ledecky-on-her-tokyo-wins-mental-health-and-gender-equality-in-sports

## MIA HAMM

Athletes for Hope. (n.d.). *Mia Hamm*. https://www.athletesforhope.org/founders-and-ambassadors/mia-hamm/

Brown, M. (2023, February 15). *LibGuides: Mia Hamm: About*. Westport Library. https://westportlibrary.libguides.com/MiaHamm

CNN programs - people in the news. (n.d.). https://edition.cnn.com/CNN/Programs/people/shows/hamm/profile.html

CNN - "Go for the Goal" - July 14, 1999. (n.d.). http://edition.cnn.com/books/beginnings/9907/Go.For.Goal/

Davis, N. (2018, October 3). *The vision of a champion is someone who is...*Medium. https://medium.com/@iamnatedavis/the-vision-of-a-champion-is-someone-who-is-bent-over-drenched-in-sweat-at-the-point-of-b94c26277e4

Garcia, N. & B. (2023, November 22). *Mia Hamm: Goals, games, and gratitude*. Apple Podcasts. https://podcasts.apple.com/es/podcast/mia-hamm-goals-games-and-gratitude/id1451565442?i=1000635658867

Hamm, M. (2005). My own words. In *eJOURNAL USA*. https://ciaotest.cc.columbia.edu/olj/gli/gli_jan2005/gli_jan2005c.pdf

Hilton, L. (n.d.). *No me in Mia*. ESPN Classic. http://www.espn.com/classic/biography/s/Hamm_Mia.html

*Mia Hamm*. (2019, September 21). Wikipedia. https://en.wikipedia.org/wiki/Mia_Hamm

Schroeck-Singh, K. (2021, March 12). *6 lessons from Mia Hamm*. Medium. https://hirekarin.medium.com/6-lessons-from-mia-hamm-a084b3ea21d9

## DANICA PATRICK

Biography.com Editors. (2021a, March 29). *Danica Patrick biography*. Biography. https://www.biography.com/athletes/danica-patrick

*Danica bio*. (n.d.). The Official Website of Danica Patrick. https://www.danicapatrick.com/danica

Danica Patrick bio and facts. (2023, February 6). rookie road. https://www.rookieroad.com/nascar/danica-patrick-bio-and-facts/

Life Stories. (2023, May 2). *Danica Patrick Interview: Most Successful Woman in American Open-Wheel Car Racing History* [Video]. YouTube. https://www.youtube.com/watch?v=UPVTzJO6yd8

Mediaplanet. (n.d.). *Former racing driver Danica Patrick talks succeeding in male-dominated fields*. Business and Tech. https://www.futureofbusinessandtech.com/empowering-our-female-truckers/former-racing-driver-danica-patrick-talks-succeeding-in-male-dominated-fields/#

Roll, R. (2018, January 29). *Danica Patrick is Pretty Intense -- Life Lessons From The World's Greatest Female Race Car Driver*. Rich Roll. https://www.richroll.com/podcast/danica-patrick/

Schabner, D. (2013, February 18). *Danica Patrick becomes first woman to take pole at Daytona 500*. ABC News. https://abcnews.go.com/blogs/headlines/2013/02/danica-patrick-becomes-first-woman-to-take-pole-at-daytona-500

Schwabel, D. (2018, January 11). *Danica Patrick's 5 secrets to living a successful and happy life*. CNBC. https://www.cnbc.com/2018/01/11/nascar-driver-danica-patricks-secrets-of-a-successful-happy-life.html

## DAME SARAH STOREY

Driving Force. (2022, April 22). *Driving Force - Season 1 - Dame Sarah Storey DBE | FULL EPISODE* [Video]. YouTube. https://www.youtube.com/watch?v=W2FnJw7vVow

Maidment, A. (2020, February 7). *Leading Manchester sporting hero launches £535k breast cancer pledge*. Manchester Evening News. https://www.manchestereveningnews.co.uk/news/greater-manchester-news/paralympian-sarah-storey-cancer-pledge-17703892

Team England. (2010, March 10). *Cycling: Storey's sights set on historic ride*. Commonwealth Games England. https://teamengland.org/news/cycling-storeys-sights-set-on-historic-ride

*World's greatest Paralympian inspires pupils*. (2021, September 23). Post. https://www.kingsmac.co.uk/news-events/latest-news/post/~board/news/post/kings-establishes-heritage-orchard-at-new-campus-1632425860407

Tucker, H. (2024, March 3). *Dame Sarah Storey DBE, on leaving a legacy of determination, resilience and triumph*. Apple Podcasts. https://podcasts.apple.com/gb/podcast/dame-sarah-storey-dbe-on-leaving-a-legacy/id1434529830?i=1000647878167

Wikipedia contributors. (2024, August 27). *Sarah Storey*. Wikipedia. https://en.wikipedia.org/wiki/Sarah_Storey

## LETICIA BUFONI

*About Leticia*. (n.d.). Leticia Bufoni. https://www.leticiabufoni.com/about#

Bufoni, L. (2021, July 23). Letter to my Dad by Leticia Buffoons | The Players'

Tribune. *The Players' Tribune.* https://www.theplayerstribune.com/posts/letter-to-my-dad-leticia-bufoni-skateboarding-olympics

Leticia Bufoni. (2023, November 24). Wikipedia. https://en.wikipedia.org/wiki/Let%C3%ADcia_Bufoni

Letícia Bufoni. (n.d.). Issuu. https://issuu.com/redbulletin.com/docs/trb_eng_cityguide_tokyo_lowres/s/13103725

*Leticia Bufoni: the female skater who conquered the world* (n.d.). Surfer Today https://www.surfertoday.com/skateboarding/leticia-bufoni-the-life-and-career-of-an-influential-female-skater

Sedghi, A. (2022, December 16). From Brazil to the world: The rise of Leticia Bufoni. Glorious Sport. https://glorioussport.com/articles/leticia-bufoni-red-bull-brazilian-skating-interview/

Tang, V. (2020, October 23). *Leticia Bufoni is boarding for breast cancer.* Red Bull. https://www.redbull.com/us-en/leticia-bufoni-boarding-for-breast-cancer

*The "GIZMO" Interviews: Leticia Bufoni.* (n.d.). https://www.thrashermagazine.com/articles/the-gizmo-interviews-leticia-bufoni/

## BETHANY HAMILTON

*Bethany Hamilton.* (2019, March 26). Wikipedia. https://en.wikipedia.org/wiki/Bethany_Hamilton

*Bethany's Story.* (n.d.). Bethany Hamilton. https://bethanyhamilton.com/biography/#

California Surf Museum. (2019, April 9). *Courageous Inspiration: Bethany Hamilton.* https://surfmuseum.org/current-exhibits/courageous-inspiration-bethany-hamilton/

Hamilton, B. (2024). *Top 60 Bethany Hamilton quotes (2024 update).* QuoteFancy. https://quotefancy.com/bethany-hamilton-quotes

Hughes, A. (2016, August 9). *What soul surfer Bethany Hamilton teaches us about tragedy, faith, and finding life's purpose.* YouAligned. https://youaligned.com/lifestyle/3-inspiring-life-lessons-can-learn-soul-surfer-bethany-hamilton/

Mayer, M. (2023, October 13). "You too can overcome": Bethany Hamilton reflects on 20th anniversary of shark attack. Great American Pure Flix. https://www.pureflix.com/insider/bethany-hamilton-reflects-20th-anniversary-shark-attack

Parsons, R. (2022, March 23). *Bethany Hamilton's "Beautifully Flawed" foundation empowers those who've suffered limb loss.* The Inertia. https://www.theinertia.com/surf/bethany-hamiltons-beautifully-flawed-foundation-empowers-those-whove-suffered-limb-loss/

Shank, S. (2021, August 23). *5 things we can learn from soul surfer: Soul Surfer movie study.* Learn in Color. https://learnincolor.com/soul-surfer-movie-study.html

Printed in Great Britain
by Amazon